THE ACCOUNTANT IN A CHANGING BUSINESS ENVIRONMENT

Papers Presented for Discussion
in the University of Florida
Distinguished Accountants Seminar Series
1970-1972

Edited by
WILLIARD E. STONE

University of Florida Press
Gainesville

UNIVERSITY OF FLORIDA ACCOUNTING SERIES NO. 8

Library of Congress Cataloging in Publication Data
Main entry under title

The accountant in the changing business environment.

"Papers presented for discussion in the University of Florida distinguished accountants seminar series, 1970-1972."
1. Accounting--Addresses, essay, lectures.
2. Accountants--United States--Addresses, essays, lectures. I. Stone, Williard E., 1910- ed.
II. Title. III. Series: Florida. University, Gainesville. Dept. of Accounting. Accounting Series, no. 8
HF5601.F55 no. 8 [HF5629] 657 72-14361
ISBN 0-8130-0378-4

Printed in U.S.A.

UNIVERSITY OF FLORIDA ACCOUNTING SERIES

No. 1 Financial and Managerial Reporting by Certified Public Accountants
62 pp., 1963 Paper, $1.50
A Collection of papers concerning the accountant's report to management, as well as financial projection through accounting.

No. 2 Annotated Bibliography of Electronic Data Processing
52 pp., 1968 Paper, $1.95
The revised edition of a comprehensive bibliography which contains entries on over 60 books and 300 articles from professional journals up to December 31, 1967.

No. 3 The American Accounting Association--Sponsored Statements of Standards for Corporate Reports, A Perspective
by Harvey T. Deinzer
52 pp., 1964 Paper, $1.25
Comparative analyses of the four major Statements of Accounting Principles issued by the American Accounting Association, in 1936, 1941, 1948, and 1957.

No. 4 Aspects of Contemporary Accounting
83 pp., 1968 Paper, $1.25
An examination of several topics related to problems encountered in contemporary accounting, such as estate planning, macro-accounting, and absolutism.

No. 5 Methodological Presuppositions in Financial Accounting Models
by Harvey T. Deinzer
99 pp., 1968 Paper, $1.95
An organization of accounting doctrines and patterns in reference to assumptions about the conditions for knowledge.

No. 6 Theory Formulations
Williard E. Stone, Editor
97 pp., 1970 Paper, $1.95
A survey of the historical development of accounting postulates and suggestions toward the development of accounting principles for specific purposes.

No. 7 Foundations of Accounting Theory
Williard E. Stone, Editor
163 pp., 1971 $6.00
A series of papers presented by twelve distinguished accounting scholars investigating both the theoretical and applied natures of accounting and providing an understanding of the total systems aspect of accounting.

PRIOR ACCOUNTING STUDIES

#1 "Financial and Managerial Reporting by Certified Public Accountants"

#2 "Annotated Bibliography of Electronic Data Processing: Updated to December 31, 1967"

#3 "The American Accounting Association--Sponsored Statements of Standards for Corporate Financial Reports--A Perspective by Harvey T. Deinzer

#4 "Aspects of Contemporary Accounting"

#5 "Methodological Presuppositions in Financial Accounting Models" by Harvey T. Deinzer

#6 "Theory Formulations"

#7 "Foundations of Accounting Theory"

Copies of all Accounting Series issues may be secured from
University of Florida Press
15 N.W. 15th Street
Gainesville, Florida 32601

Contents

Introduction

It is very early in the present decade, and therefore foolhardy to attempt to evaluate the role of the accountant in the 1970's. Hopefully this decade will bring solutions to the many new problems facing the accountant as a heritage of the 1960's. The business environment of the United States during the 1960's was characterized by changes of great magnitude. The accounting profession, because it had achieved a large measure of stability since its last great shake-up of the 1930's, felt the weight of these changes to a greater extent that most of the other segments of the business community.

Tried and tested doctrines such as the cost basis concept were seriously questioned and some appear to be crumbling. Al Rappaport's paper is concerned with the effects of inflation on the cost basis concept, with particular emphasis upon the utilities industry.

Another comfortable pattern, which accountants are beginning to reluctantly admit may need change, is their objectivity requirement that accountants deal only with measurements that can be quantified with a high degree of certainty. Campfield's and Churchill's papers explore the accountant's role in the measurement of social change. Meeting this challenge will require new concepts of measurement and a willingness to deal with uncertainty.

Livingstone's paper explores the accountant's use of behavioral science and organizational theory concepts as a framework for the design of information systems capable of meeting management's stepped-up requirements of the 1970's.

The four papers cover a wide range of the current problems facing the accounting profession. We hope that they will prove to be as stimulating to the readers as they were to the faculty and graduate students who attended the seminars.

Financial support for research on the paper of Alfred Rappaport was in part provided by Illinois Bell Telephone.

The Accountant's Opportunity for Participating in the Solution of Socioeconomic Problems

Traditionally, businessmen (and the professional people who counsel and service them) have conducted their activities pursuant to the notion that business management has a first responsibility to society to profitably allocate and use economic resources. Moreover, as Peter Drucker has often expressed the idea, businessmen have traditionally acted out a belief that they had an all encompassing moral responsibility for organized economic progress.

In the recent two decades the accelerated change in the physical and social environment of our country has evoked demands from society for business and professional people to take the leadership reins in improving the quality of life in this country.

I will attempt in this paper to: (1) sort out and briefly describe a few major social problems warranting urgent attention; (2) suggest some general problem solving approaches; and (3) predict some probable directions that accountants may pursue in pushing back the frontiers of measuring and evaluating social programs.

Anyone who would attempt to predict the future has two strikes against him to start. But at least the would-be predictor should be as positive as possible. There comes to mind the story of the sultan who called a soothsayer and commanded him: "Predict my future." The soothsayer looked into his crystal ball and said,"Sir, I have bad news. All of your relatives will die before you." The sultan had the soothsayer executed. Then he called in another soothsayer and commanded him: "Tell me my future." This soothsayer gazed long into his crystal ball and exclaimed: "Sir, I have great news for you. You will outlive all your relatives." And the sultan said, "Reward that man handsomely." To predict in today's world we are faced with a somewhat similar challenge: we must be sensitive to the choice of words and be careful as to their implications.

Before embarking on the voyage of predictions and challenges it might be useful background to examine briefly some features of the current environment in which business and professional people are expected to act wisely and timely.

THE CONTEMPORARY DECISION-MAKING ENVIRONMENT

The first and most notable observation about the current scene is the rate of change taking place in society. The technological changes which have occurred as a steady parade since the late 1940s are but the beginning of a continuum of basic change. All of the key factors making for change are at work to produce even greater change in the future. For example, the population explosion about which we shall discourse later, is likely to place excruciating demands upon the business and professional community to find quick solutions to problems of better provision of goods and services to the burgeoning society.

It is also relevant to the first observation to point out the incidence of scale of education in today's world. The ideal of mass education on a high level is no longer just a dream but a rapidly approaching reality. This increasingly more educated society of ours is becoming more mobile and information and communication devices of all shapes and kinds are multiplying in a way to cause the more educated and more mobile population to clamor like Dickens' Oliver Twist for more and more goods and services. All of this requires an accelerated and better managed rate of technological and sociological change if the innovations and discoveries necessary to accommodate the demands of this greatly enlarged society are to be forthcoming.

The second notable observation we should make about the managerial decision environment is the growth of techniques, methodologies, and media for helping managers to make decisions. Some of the people who have worked on scientific decision methods have gathered all of these under the heading "Decision Theory." This is erroneous labeling since the bundle of techniques and methods is not a single, consistent theory of how to make decisions but rather a collection of techniques, methods, and media for weighing and evaluating various factors underlying two or more possible courses of action. Suffice it to say at this point, however, that all so-called "Decision Theory" has an avowed common purpose of furnishing decision makers with reliable information and means for attaining their goals and objectives.

A third background observation is that decisions, especially at the top levels of complex social and economic structures, often involve considerable uncertainty and risks. Moreover, a large number of decisions required in the present milieu are unprogrammed, i.e., are novel, unstructured and for which few precise precedents exist. Therefore, in a complicated and even changing society where there are competing demands for relatively scarce resources it is abundantly clear that decision making in today's tormented world calls for the very best of leadership and management talent, vision, and sensitivity to the frailties of a large part of humanity.

Now that we have commented upon social problems in kaleidoscope, a fitting sequence is to examine selected problems in greater detail. Two overriding problem areas, viz. population and technology, are discussed in the body of the paper. Four subordinate areas; poverty, citizen rights and opportunities, education, and health are analyzed in a matrix of problem indicia and suggested solutions as set forth in an Appendix to this paper.

TWO KEY PROBLEMS REQUIRING URGENT MANAGEMENT ACTION

All of the major management problems of societal change could well be telescoped into these two: (1) Managing the burgeoning and mobile population, and (2) Managing ideological and technological change. Let me talk first of three aspects of the population problem, namely: (i) hunger, (ii) rate of growth and concentration of population, and (iii) consequences of urban congestion.

Lord C. P. Snow, eminent British novelist, speaking at Westminster College in November, 1968, despaired that the United States will, before the year 2000 (maybe as soon as 10 years), be surrounded by a sea of famine unless this country, possibly with aid from a few other countries, takes 3 steps:

1. Make massive grants of food to poor countries.
2. Give massive money and technical aid to the poor countries (perhaps as much as 20% of the U.S. GNP for the next 15 years).
3. Aid the poor countries in attaining increased efficiency in food production as well as concurrent control of population growth.

The United States is currently a nation of about 200 million. At the current level growth rate of about 2½% or 5 million per year there would be about 350 million people by the year 2000. We are also a nation becoming fast urbanized and "megalopolisezed." In the early 1800's only about10% of the population lived in cities and towns. By the 1960's this concentration had increased to 70% in cities and towns occupying about 1% of the total land of the country. By the year 2000 it has been predicted that about 90% of the population will be concentrated in cities and towns on about 2% of the land, excluding Alaska.

Further in thinking about the trend to urbanization and megalopolises, we should be reminded that the sheer size of population enclaves will pose logistics and housekeeping problems of indeterminate complexity. Herman Kahn, a member of the Commission of the Year 2000 of the American Academy of Arts and Sciences, has been quoted many times as predicting that by the year 2000 there will be at least three megalopolises in the United States. One of these will extend from Washington to Boston and contain almost one-quarter of the American people. Another, centered around the Great Lakes, may stretch from Chicago to Pittsburgh and north to Canada--thereby including Detroit, Toledo, Cleveland, Akron, Buffalo, and Rochester. This megalopolis seems likely to contain more than one-eighth of the U. S. population. A Pacific megalopolis that will presumably stretch from Santa Barbara, California, to San Diego, might contain more than one-sixteenth of the population. Mr. Kahn forsees that these three megalopolises will contain "roughly one-half" of the total United States population, including the overwhelming majority of the most technologically and scientifically advanced, and prosperous and creative elements.

The foregoing points up the fact that a constantly increasing and congested population is more likely than not to be restive and explosive. The recent tragic civil disorders in our urban centers are a clarion warning that the very best management talent from both the public and the private sectors will need to confront the issues squarely and promptly. Here listed are some of the consequences of the unresolved handling of basic urban problems:

Constantly accelerating welfare dependency.
Increasing criminal incidents and disregard for established laws.
Increasing educational dropouts and deterioration of the quality of education in many inner city schools.
Deterioration of housing in the inner cities.

Increasing incidence of disease and health hazards.
Increasing air and water pollution
Declining quantity and quality and increasing cost of public transportation.

Now let us turn to the second telescoped macroscopic management problem, i.e., managing ideological and technological change. Catalogued below are some indicators of the staggering rate of change that has been and is going on about us:

College enrollment by 1970 was estimated to be about 9 million. The National Science Foundation estimates that 90% of all scientists who ever lived were alive in 1966.
In 1940 less than $1 billion was spent on research and development; in 1968, about $16 billion; and in 1975, an estimated $30 billion will be spent.
The gestation period for major product innovation is shortening significantly; e.g.,

1. *The key-driven desk calculator.*--Took roughly 80 years to evolve from its crude beginning in the 19th century to a truly useful device.
2. *Punched card tabulating machines.*--Required only 40 years from beginning to present usefulness.
3. *Computers.*--Required just 20 years from discoveries out of World War II to the threshold of reliability of the 1960's.
4. *So-called 3rd generation computers.*--Large memories, random access, on-line and time sharing--were invented less than 10 years ago and are now operative.
5. *Photography.*--Took 115 years from its first conception to first commercially useful form.
6. *The telephone.*--Gestatory span was 56 years; but the comparable span for videography was only 6 years.

Mathematics and systems theory are being used in an increasing degree for determining mix for outputs or products, economic order level, inventory location, and other means of optimizing the use of resources.

The most useful conclusion to be drawn from the foregoing recital is that technological and ideological change could very well double or triple during the 1970's.

Dr. Anthony J. Wiener, Chairman, Research Management Council, the Hudson Institute, testified recently before a Congressional committee on his research into the anticipated social impact of anticipated technological changes. Among other things, he informed the committee that he and an associate had prepared in 1967 a list of 100 technological innovations likely to occur during the last third of the 20th century.[1] Here are but a few examples of what Dr. Wiener thinks is ahead for us before the year 2000:

New sources of power for fixed installation (e.g., magneto hydrodynamic, thermionic and thermoelectric, and radio-active).
Major reduction in heriditary and congenital defects.
New or improved uses of the ocean for extraction of minerals, and controlled sources of energy.
Use of nuclear explosives for excavation and mining, generation of power, creation of high temperature-high pressure environments, and/or as a source of neutrons or other radiation.

Practical use of direct electronic communication with and stimulation of the brain.
Human hibernation for relatively extensive periods (for months and possibly years).
Completely automated grocery and department stores.

It is also useful to note some of Dr. Wiener's 25 "less likely but important possibilities" for innovation as well as a couple of his "far out possibilities."[2]

LESS LIKELY POSSIBILITIES

1. Artifical growth of new limbs and organs (either in situs or for later transplant).
2. Direct augmentation of human mental capacity by the mechanical or the electrical interconnection of the brain with a computer.
3. Effective chemical or biological treatment for most mental illnesses.
4. Automated highways.

FAR OUT POSSIBILITIES

1. Lifetime immunization against practically all diseases.
2. Substantial lunar or planetary bases or colonies.

SUGGESTED PROBLEM SOLVING APPROACHES FOR MANAGERS

It is often not overly difficult to state the issues, but getting at the answers is something else again. Suppose we discuss in inverse order the two major problems raised earlier and suggest some directions for managing the change in technology and ideology.

Because we are a better educated and more flexible people, managements themselves have been compelled to be:

1. "open minded" and attuned to managing the situation of people vis-a-vis machines.
2. attuned to organizing and motivating people and organization to achieve well defined and rewarding goals.
3. social service results and responsibility oriented.

Also, because like the mountain climber who climbs because the mountain is there, managers have learned to put information and production technology to use because these, too, are there. In addition to the industrial model building and simulation mentioned in the preceding section, managers especially in the public sector are intensifying the use of systems analysis and planning-programming-budgeting (PPB) techniques to accomplish better allocation of resources to the solution of "people problems."

In thinking about the traumas of management in its efforts to control change, we could do worse than follow the admonition of Marshall McLuhan, the oracle of socio-politicism, who declares: "As the age of information demands the simultaneous use of all of our faculties we discover that we are most at leisure when we are most intensely involved."[3]

Now to turn to suggested approaches and ideas about solving the problems that have arisen mostly because of the burgeoning and mobility aspects of population. Dwight Ink, Assistant Director for Executive Management, Bureau of the Budget, in a thoughtful article about a year ago identified the "people problems" as old as man and as new as space technology. But he also averred that management of action programs in this area presents no more strange and exotic difficulties than would be encountered in the management of complex activities anywhere in the private or public domain.[4]

The major efforts to solve the population proliferation problems have emanated primarily from the Federal Government through grants to States and local governments. Because of this approach it is useful to set forth capsule information about Federal grants-in-aid. First, these statistics indicate the magnitude of this form of Federal assistance:[5]

DOLLAR DIMENSIONS (IN BILLIONS)

Fiscal Year 1946		0.9
Fiscal Year 1956		3.6
Fiscal Year 1966		$12.8
Fiscal Year 1970 by Federal Department or Agency:		
Health, Education, and Welfare	12.3	
Transportation	5.1	
Housing and Urban Development	2.2	
Economic Opportunity Programs	1.3	
Agriculture	1.8	
All others	1.9	
TOTAL		24.6

PROGRAM AND ADMINISTRATIVE DIMENSIONS

• Estimates of the number of programs	170 to 220
• Number of Federal appropriations used in financing programs	400
• Administration units:	
Federal agencies	21
Major Washington, D.C. bureaus	150
Federal agency field offices	400
• State and local government participation	
States	50
Local governments	92,000

Bureau of the Budget estimates place the dollar total of Federal grants at the $60 billion level by 1975.

In the massive bureacracies that are American public enterprise there are bound to be overlaps, inadequacies, and non-responsive methods and procedures. The present writer has discussed some of these deterrents to efficiency in greater detail in another paper.[6] A summary is, however, useful to the present paper.

OVERLAPS

Funds for job recruiting can be obtained from nine manpower program sources; for adult basic education from ten sources; for prevocational training and skills training from ten sources; and for work experience from five sources. On-the-job training can be financed under nine programs. Eligibility rules, application procedures, allocation formulas, expiration dates, and contracting arrangements vary considerably between programs.

A city which wanted to build a river-front park found money available under four different Federal programs--the Open Space Program, the Outdoor-Recreation Program, the Beautification Program, and the Parks-Development Program. Even after making the choice that appeared to offer an advantage, the city was still uncertain as to whether it had made the best choice.

Another city found that it required four different Federal grants to build a center which included physical and mental health facilities, a library, indoor and outdoor recreation programs, and a family counseling service.

INADEQUACIES AND INFLEXIBILITIES

States and local governments are allowed little discretion in allocating grant funds according to some scale of needs priority. Federal agencies often bypass State governments in making grants to local governments, and thus contribute to impairment of State government planning and control. Coordination between Federal agencies in administering similar programs and grants is weak or completely lacking. A multiplicity of Federal requirements for applying for grants and for accounting and reporting use of grant money has caused an inordinate and overlapping amount of paper work. Multiple audits by various units of government as well as by public accountants tend to interfere with timely and efficient grant administration, particularly at the grantee field level.

Although there have been various programs to improve the management of "people programs" there still is a sizeable gap between the grandeur of Federal policy pronouncements and the "bolts and nuts" realities of day-to-day administration and implementation of programs. The writer elsewhere made some modest, if perhaps irreverent, proposals for solution to the problems of diseconomy.[7] A summary is given here:

One Federal agency should be designated as *single manner* for all aid programs that pertain to a category of functional area. For example, all grants that have to do with education programs should be "managed" (i.e., administered after the initial application, review, funding had been accomplished) by the Office of Education in the Department of Health, Education, and Welfare. Similarly, job and skills training grant programs should be "managed" by the appropriate agency within the Department of Labor.

State and local governments need to first improve their administration of their tax assessment and collection and related expenditure of funds, and corollarily, need to adopt modern methods of planning,programming, and budgeting.

Recipients of Federal grants should be authorized greater discretion in determining the relative priority of their needs and the most effective way to use Federal aid funds.

National and regional clearing houses need to be set up to furnish timely information and models on the best ways for Federal agencies to identify States and local governments needy of Federal financial assistance.

There needs to be concerted effort among the grant partners to clarify the roles of cities vis-a-vis the Federal Government in specific grant programs; to appropriately adjust differences from State to State in the relationship between city and State under Federal grants; and, to minimize the differences in Federal benefits granted to various geographic regions.

Finally, there needs to be a massive coalition of the public sector and the private sector (total and inter-disciplinary) in funding and administering programs such as slum eradication that cut across multi-forms of government, organization, tools, and disciplines.

CHALLENGES AND POTENTIAL FOR PROFESSIONAL ADVISORS TO MANAGEMENT

One could say as some of the political poets are prone to do that the future is "bursting with the promise of endless tomorrows." However, realism constrains us to observe that potential and opportunity come wrapped in a more austere and rigorous form. Two general observations in this regard are especially useful at this stage: (1) the numerous techniques and the vast knowledge that must be applied to the solution of today's complexities require a large number and variety of specialists, e.g., behaviorists, economists, mathematicians, engineers, accountants, lawyers, budget analysts, and so on, and (2) these specialists must learn to work together and communicate adequately across narrow disciplinary lines.

Accountants and auditors have long served business managements as key counsellors on financial information systems problems and related matters. There seems to be abundant precedent to support the notion that accountants and auditors can extend the boundaries of this expertise. David Linowes has presented an interesting tabulation and rationalization in exhortation to accountants to extend their measurement theory and technique into social areas requiring quantitative measurement.[8]

One of the major public accounting firms has presented a fairly extended description of the way in which it utilized the talents of an interdisciplinary team to build a mathematical model for use by a large city to secure the most efficient allocation of its resources in its war on poverty.[9] Patently, comparable models could be developed for applicability to other areas of social improvement such as health, education, housing and so on.

A most ambitious study by a committee of the American Accounting Association included among other ideas a suggestion that accountants might be called upon for the collection and reporting of data which could be used by interested parties in the evaluation of individual enterprises' contributions toward maximizing social welfare. The study states as an example a supposition that businessmen might be called upon to report information concerning:

1. The feeling of "well-offness" of its employees, possibly through use of some standardized attitude measurement technique.
2. The degree to which safety standards are met, possibly through use of some indices of "safeness" such as accident-free days of operations, level of plant illumination, and the like.
3. The economic power of specific business entities, i.e., rating of industrial concentration.[10]

Over and beyond the specific extensions of technical expertise such as described above, accountants as part of a social leadership stratum can further make their presence felt in the big social arena of life.

Here are but two of many broad areas in which contributions can be made individually and collectively:

> Do more planned study and thinking about where science, technology, and directed behaviorism is leading the nation. Accountants as experts in internal controls should devise specific means and procedures for controlling the planning and application of change in a way to best ensure that change will be managed for the well-being of the maximum feasible number of people.
>
> Become more active in proposing to and working with Government and private organizations to organize and adapt research and related scientific achievements to the improvement of the human environment. In short, help adapt the market-oriented applied-research model to the solution of non-market problems.

CONCLUSION

To sum up briefly what has been attempted in this paper:

1. *THE ENVIRONMENT OF RAPID CHANGE*

The technological, demographical, and ideological changes of recent decades are occurring at a bewildering rate and complexion. Alvin Toffler writing in *Horizon*, Summer, 1965, stated it well:

> The fact is . . . even the most educated people today operate on the assumption that society is relatively static. At best they attempt to plan by making simple straightline projections of present trends . . . . We have no objects, no friends, no relatives, no works of art, no music or literature that originate in the future. We have as it were, no heritage of the future . . . the result is unreadiness to meet the future when it arrives. In short, 'future shock.'

Perhaps the most valuable role for business and professional leaders is to help cushion the effect of future shock.

2. *ADAPTATION OF THE NEW TECHNOLOGY AND EFFICIENT RESOURCES MANAGEMENT*

The overall task of management can be stated simply as one of putting together, directing, and controlling a fluid package of people and physical resources to accomplish some predetermined output at an attainable "least cost." The acid test of a good manager is a demonstration by him of capacity to make timely decisions and ability to get these decisions translated into desirable action and outputs. Information and decision-facilitating techniques, methods, and media when soundly formulated and wisely used by managers and their advisers obviously can form a basis for more informed and more timely planning, decision and control.

3. *THE ROLE OF THE PROFESSIONAL COUNSELLORS AND SPECIALISTS*

A single human mind, unassisted by others, cannot possible weigh and evaluate the manifold complexities and the wide range of information that concerns modern day activities of business and government entities. A manager must call upon professionals and other specialists if he expects to make useful decisions. Accountants and auditors are but one of many professionals available. The decision-facilitating role of the various professionals or specialists is assured provided that they act rationally in presenting the decision maker with a range of well thought out alternatives. There is always the danger to be guarded against that some counsellors to managers will operate in the somewhat arrogant belief that their favorite techniques can produce precise and automatic decisions.

4. *AN EPILOGUE*

The words of an anonymous poet might serve as lodestar for anyone committed to furtherance of the public welfare, "We may well get to the moon, but that is not very far. The greatest distance a man has to cover lies within him."

NOTES

1. Senate Resolution 78--*To Establish a Select Senate Committee on Technology and the Human Environment*--Print of the Subcommittee of Intergovernmental Relations, Committee on Government Operations, U.S. Government Printing Office, Washington, D.C., 1969, pp 34-36.
2. *Ibid*, pp 37-38.
3. Quoted in *Management Review*, September 1969, p 59.
4. Dwight A. Ink, "A Management Crises for the New President: People Programs", *Public Administration Review,* Vol. 28, No. 6, Nov/Dec 1968.
5. *Report on Survey of Financial Administration of Federal Grants-in-Aid to States and Local Governments* - Unpublished report of the Joint Financial Management Improvement Program, September 1969, p 9.
6. W. L. Campfield, "Administration of Grants: Is the Federalist Partnership Synergistic or Symbiotic?" *Business and Government Review*, Vol. 10, No. 4, July/August 1969, p 8-9.
7. *Ibid*, p 11.
8. David F. Linowes, "Socio-Economic Accounting", *The Journal of Accountancy*, November, 1968, pp 37-42.
9. Robert Beyer, "The Modern Management Approach to a Program of Social Improvement", *The Journal of Accountancy*, March, 1969, pp 37-46.
10. *Committee on Non-Financial Measures of Effectiveness*, American Accounting Association, Unpublished draft report, July 1, 1970, pp 45-46.

APPENDIX

AN APPROACH TO ANALYSIS OF KEY SOCIO-ECONOMIC PROBLEMS

A Matrix of Indicia and Goals

PROBLEM AREAS AND INDICIA / *GOALS AND GUIDES*

PROBLEM AREAS AND INDICIA

1. *Poverty* (related unemployment, hunger, etc.)

25 million poor people in 1969 per Social Security Administration estimates. About 8 million poor, roughly 4% of total population lived in households headed by person 65 years or older (6 million) or headed by persons who are disabled (2 million).

Population concentration in urban centers accelerating and adding to employment, housing, education, transportation, and health problems:

1. 1960 census showed 70% of population in cities and towns; year 2000 prediction is that 90% of population will be in towns and cities, on 2% of total land (excluding Alaska).
2. From 1940 to 1960, although the population increase in the several large metropolitan complexes was 55%, the component increases were:
   a. In central cities - 27% increase.
   b. Outside central cities - 102% increase.

GOALS AND GUIDES

1. *Poverty Elimination*

Many plans advanced, e.g. guaranteed income, negative income tax, family allowances, wage supplements, etc.

Doubtless, the optimal solution would consist of a combination of continued economic growth and operation of the free market system, added efforts at training and educating hard-core unemployed, elimination of prejudicial employment practices, and changes and improvements in income maintenance programs.

Also, probable changes toward a national system or standards for welfare payments for aged, blind, disabled, etc.

PROBLEM AREAS AND INDICIA

2. *Inequalities in Opportunities and Rights of Citizenry*

Prejudices and inequities based on race, religion, and country of origin are the most prevalent and continuing problems.

Biases based on sex causes periodic upsurges in protests and re-examination.

The "Youth Revolt" focused heavily on:

1. Voting rights
2. Right of representation in decision making apparatus of institutions of higher education
3. Restricting concepts and mechanisms of military institutions, e.g., do away with "unjust wars"; have more equitable draft system; abolish campus ROTC, etc.

GOALS AND GUIDES

2. *Re-emphasis and Guarantee of Constitutional and Moral Rights to all Citizenry*

Primal need to upgrade the quality of administration of legal and other administrative machinery, i.e., *substantive enforcement of the major laws and administrative directives already on the books.*

Ensure "maximum feasible participation" as an option for all of the underprivileged (a, b, c, categories stated under Problems opposite) in planning of programs which affect them.

Strong personal example by leaders in government, business, labor, education, and religion toward creating a better climate for equality of opportunity.

PROBLEM AREAS AND INDICIA

3. *Inadequacies and Financial Difficulties of the Educational System*

Proliferation of number of schools and of persons seeking education has resulted in:

1. Inadequate financing
2. Increasing gap between quantity of courses and quality of education.

GOALS AND GUIDES

3. *Upgrading and Updating the Educational System*

Since the public secondary school system is catalytic to the quality of American education, urgent coordinated Government (Federal-State local) and private sector action needed to provide adequate continuing funding.

Great controversies regarding the relevance and responsiveness of educational programs to the current and future needs of populace.

Paucity of research and forward preparation for instruction needed in years ahead.

Lack of aequate remedial instruction for the underprivileged.

Universities, foundations, and other institutions need to participate more actively and comprehensively in the process of education at all levels.

Increased funding and effort needed in research into the nature of learning and innovation.

Assurance of equal opportunity to quality education for all who meet pertinent minimum entrance requirements.

4. *Inadequacy of Health and Medicare Care*

Inadequate facilities and staff cause:

1. large number of people without adequate services (even those who can pay).
2. many instances of failure to use existing facilities with maximum effectiveness.

Present economics of medical care not assuring allocation of available services where needed most e.g., in rural slums and urban ghettos.

Inadequacy in planning and research in respect to:

1. Identification of and assigning priorities to disease and health impairment prevention and cure.
2. Long-range planning for provision of adequate funds, facilities, and personnel.

4. *Improving and Expanding the Medical Care System*

Investment and experimentation in new ways for organizing, financing, and delivering medical care.

Greater emphasis on providing adequate care to indigents, elderly, handicapped, and children.

Coordinated effort of the public and private sectors to bring the same kind of operating efficiency utilized by "manufacturing industry" to the "medical care industry".

The Accountant's Role in Social Responsibility

ACCOUNTING AND THE QUALITY OF LIFE

The changing nature of the American economic and social climate is causing a reexamination of the Nation's goals and reassessment and questioning of the roles that should be played by different institutions and organizations. At the national level, there is a marked shift from concern only with economic performance and growth to a balance of quantity with quality and an allocation of the Nation's resources towards correcting social problems and achieving social goals. The factors identified as producing these shifts are varied but seem to center on (1) a level of material affluence vis-a-vis the 1930's, which permits us to be concerned about things beyond basic food, clothing, and shelter; (2) the development of institutions that have achieved great successes in some areas (GM and NASA) and therefore can be expected to achieve even greater success in others; (3) a world of growing population in which the effects of people, institutions, or governments upon one another are clearly perceived and often of awesome potential; and (4) a realization that our resources are limited and we must assign priorities.[1]

Along with the change in emphasis has come the realization that with continued increase in complexity, the achievement of social goals requires the development of social conditions and measures of performance to assist in evaluating specific programs, developing a balance sheet or system of social accounts, and setting goals and priorities[Land, 1971].

Concern with social issues is not limited to our national government. It focuses on all institutions and chief among them business. As the producer of most of the Nation's goods and services, business is affected by any change in national priorities. The concern for social goals, for correcting social inequities, for the community, the environment, and the quality of life affects business establishments in even more important ways. The Committee for Economic Development puts the matter this way:

> Today it is clear that the terms of the contract between society and business are, in fact, changing in substantial and important

> ways. Business is being asked to assume broader responsibilities to society than ever before and to serve a wider range of human values. Business enterprises, in effect, are being asked to contribute more to the quality of American life than just supplying quantities of goods and services. In as much as business exists to serve society, its future will depend on the quality of management's response to the changing expectations of the public [CED, 1971, p.16].

It is unclear how business can, or should, respond to the social responsibilities society is placing on it and it is unclear what the exact extent and nature of these responsibilities really are. But evidence surrounds us that there is "a new willingness to speak up, a challenge to authority (not a rejection, but a demand for bonafides other than titles and salaries), a demand for a better balance between man and nature, a new awareness of human as opposed to material values, the insistence on a bigger and better piece of the decision making action--all these, and many more are being isolated, identified, and analyzed [Bauer and Fenn, 1972, p.15]. The exact future of the corporation's social responsibility is open to question; that it *will* be held more responsible by law, by pressure, or by choice is beyond doubt.

To deal with the new and shifting responsibilities put upon it, management needs to know not only what is expected of it but what it can and is doing to meet these expectations--what resources will be required, what effects corporate actions will have, what are the costs, and, hopefully, what are the benefits. Determining these however, requires information and as Eli Goldston, President of Boston's Eastern Gas and Fuel Associates, states, "Quantification is the guts of the problem because if you can't measure it you can't do anything about it."[2] But measurement in the arena of social actions and social requirements involves concepts and methods that have not yet been developed. Steps have been taken to develop social measurement systems but they remain a challenge to social scientists, accountants, and others at both the National and the enterprise level. That accountants are expected to be involved has been stated by business leaders;[3] that accountants should direct their efforts towards social accounting and how they might begin to do so is the subject of this paper.[4]

SOCIAL MEASUREMENT

NATIONAL LEVEL

A great deal of attention has been directed towards measuring social conditions and social progress. By far the most developed statistics concern economic development and are embodied in the National Income Accounts. The great usefulness of this economic accounting framework has prompted those interested in broadening national priorities and goals to advocate the development of a system of social indicators and social schema to encompass a broader range of social conditions than Gross National Product--a wide range of conditions which are viewed under the general heading of the *Quality of Life*.[5]

In 1966 the President of the United States initiated preliminary steps toward supplementing his Economic Report. This resulted in the publication of *Towards a Social Report* which covered such issues as: health and illness, social mobility, our physical environment, income and poverty, public order, safety, learning, science and art, and participation and alienation [HEQ, 1969]. A number of writers, scientists and others have advocated a system of social accounts.[6] An extensive literature has developed in this field[7] and Senators Mondale and Harris have introduced in the U.S. Congress a bill which, if passed, would establish a council of Social Advisors with a charge similar to that of the council of Economic Advisors.

The state of social indicators is far from being resolved. While many people expound on their need[8] others caution that there is much work yet to be done and that the analogy with the National Income Accounts is dangerous.[9] In essence their argument is that the value of the National Income Accounts lies first in the conceptual framework which underlies it and ties its various parts together and second in a measuring system which permits these parts to be combined. Sheldon and Freeman [1970, pp. 102-103] argue that there is no social theory even of a tentative nature capable of defining the variables of a social system and the interrelations between them, that there is a major problem in measures that can't add and subtract "apples and oranges or cancer and rapes", and these are requisite to a system of social accounts. They do, however, argue that "the social indicator movement can contribute to the more modest and realistic goals of (1) improved descriptive reporting, (2) analysis of social change, and (3) predictions of future social events and social life" [Land, 1971, p.322]. In this latter vein a number of advances have been made in measuring social phenomena and constructing models of underlying institutions and processes. The use of victimization surveys in understanding and preventing crime is one example.[10]

Much has been done since the early 1960's in improving our understanding of social processes and in social measurement. Much still remains to be done, however, at both the conceptual and operational level. Accounting has contributed a great deal to measurement of the firm and the double-entry schema has served national economic concerns very well. It is perhaps time for accountants to become a factor in the social indicator movement.

ENTERPRISE LEVEL

As we have seen, business is faced with a changing social climate in which it is being asked to take on responsibilities that are broader than profit-maximization. There is, however, little guidance and considerable lack of unanimity on what these corporate responsibilities should be and how far they should be extended.

Business has, of course, responded to social demands. Well over 1500 corporations "have established company foundations to devote continuous and more professional attention to the philanthropic area, ..." [CED, 1971, p.41]; Quaker Oats, for example, put a manufacturing facility in Danville, Illinois only after the city passed an open-housing ordinance at the company's "suggestion;" many banks have established programs to finance minority and ghetto businesses; and, perhaps less voluntarily, minority hiring and training policies and pollution controls have been instituted. Some in our society want business to do more; some want it to do less.

Arguments are made that management should not substitute its own judgements for those of others; that it should maximize profit within the bounds laid down by society and let government, social institutions and the people themselves deal with the non-economic issues.[11]

Others argue that the market mechanism is imperfect, that it does not embody all the costs to produce socially rational decisions, particularly on the use and misuse of the environment,[12] and thus management is forced to balance "pure economics" with social considerations. The argument continues that this is of increasing importance as goals other than economic growth receive higher priority.

The different attitudes result in pressures on business to behave in a more socially responsible way through laws that prescribe or poscribe actions, e.g. pollution and employment; forces in the market-place, e.g. consumer action and action by investment groups; influence through ownership; or more direct pressures ranging from reason, through publicity to confrontation. These pressures in one way or another are directed towards guiding business to make more "socially relevant decisions."

Responding to these pressures is not made easier by our measuring system for "the concepts of growth and profit as measured by traditional balance sheets and profit-and-loss statements are too narrow to reflect what many modern corporations are trying to do." [Andrews, 1971 (a), p. 1][13] But social measurement apart from the formal economic-based accounting framework gives little aid to the executive. Let us look first at what is being done at the corporate level and then consider some further ways to assist managerial decision-making.

SOCIAL MEASUREMENT IN BUSINESS

Measuring the social performance of business organizations is being done both by the business firms themselves and by outside agencies. Some of these outside groups deal with one issue or with one organization (e.g. Campaign G.M.) others deal with a number of firms over a considerable period of time. The former have characteristics quite particular to their purpose and their situation and hence are of less general interest to us in our focus on broad methodology. Let us look then only at the latter.

OUTSIDE AGENCY MEASUREMENTS

The Dreyfus Third Century Fund was registered in 1971 with the purpose of investing in companies which, in the opinion of management, have demonstrated concern for improving the quality of life in America. The Fund is concentrating its initial attention on three areas: equality of employment opportunity, ecology, and product purity and safety. Its methods are confidential but it is developing a complex weighing scheme for evaluating companies and comparing them on a relative basis in their own industry.

Among the factors they look for are:

- Company review procedures on the performance of operating division heads which consider not only financial contribution but social concerns.
- The Firms EEO-1 report which they request from management. (The report is filed with the Equal Employment Opportunities Commission which is held confidential and published on an aggragate basis periodically.) Minority members in management.

A second fund, the Social Demensions Fund, Inc., looks toward seeking capital appreciation while limiting investments to those companies which are responding to the changing social dimensions of the times. This fund is concerned with consumerism; minority employment, training, and advancement, and general minority relations, community involvement; pollution control; employee safety and other working conditions and benefits; and corporate giving. Neither fund mentioned defense contracting or investment in South Africa.

"Representatives of both funds strongly reject the notion that there is a trade-off between social responsibility and profitability. This is contrary to the public view of the funds, as portrayed in the press, as offering the socially responsible investor who is willing to forego some profits a place to put his money" [Bauer and Fenn, 1972, p.71]. An argument in support of the funds' position comes from an analysis of the paper industry where a high correlation was established between good environmental performance, (by paper industry standards) and profits. The analysis also argues that the cause runs in the right direction [Bragdon and Marlin, 1971].[14]

Some counter research on the profitability of social concern showed that the exclusion from the Princeton University portfolio of companies doing business in South Africa would have lowered the rate of return in the portfolio by 3% by eliminating Polaroid, IBM and Xerox [Burton and Quandt, 1971].

On a different level, the National Council of Churches is accumulating data on corporate responsibility in five areas: the environment; consumer health; welfare and safety; foreign investments; military procurement and production; minorities and women. The Council gathers data and compiles data from other sources to form a Corporate Information Center. Its purpose is to exert moral suasion on churches and other interested groups to affect corporate behavior directly and to influence the investment policies of foundations, mutual funds, etc.

Another group is the Council on Economic Priorities which publishes a bi-monthly newsletter "Economic Priorities Report" and has produced two books, *Efficiency in Death* [CEP, 1970] and *Paper Profits* (to be published by the MIT Press)--the latter forming the basis for the Bragdon and Marlin study referred to above. The areas of concern of the Council are: minority hiring and training, and help in the minority community; military contracting; impact of corporations on countries abroad; and political area. It deliberately is not considering such issues as consumerism and job safety which it regards as adequately handled by others [Bauer and Fenn, 1972, p.77]. The methodology varies by area of concern. Military contracting is studied by plowing through Pentagon documents; Minority problems by talking with black "headhunters" and analyzing the EEO-I report when obtained. In pollution they talk with experts at all levels relative to the state of the art of the industry and then send very detailed questionnaires to specific company personnel. They report increasing cooperation from the firms they study--"particularly as the press calls attention to companies reluctant to cooperate" [Bauer and Fenn, 1972, p.79].

The above efforts by those outside the corporation to assess its social performance have been described to indicate the directions social measurement is taking and to underline the need for developing its methodology further.

CORPORATION MEASUREMENTS

A number of companies have developed social policies and are attempting to measure their performance against them. The term "social audit" has grown up around such measurements where corporate actions are being compared to some norm of social performance, even where the norm is primarily subjective. Some of these social audits have been documented and provide insight into the problem of social measurement.

One corporation involved in food service, vending machines, publication distribution, "newsstand supplies", etc. approached the problem of assessing how well it was meeting its responsibilities by establishing a Committee on Social Responsibilities consisting of four members of the Board of Directors, two "insiders" and two "outsiders."

The Committee addressed six segments of the business:

1. Employment and Training
   The workforce composition and the rank attained by blacks, women, ex-convicts, and the physically handicapped.
2. Environment
   Originally not viewing itself as a pollutor, the Committee found that the company was one of the largest "dishwashers" in the country. It was concerned with its paper and container waste, its discharge of detergents, its paper waste from "out of date" publications, and the garbage from its feeding operations.
3. Consumerism
   The company had long been sensitive to the quality and purity of its food products. The audit found (1) a subsidiary had sold some bowls for "marketing premiums" that had high lead content and had to be called back, (2) some of its periodicals bordered on "pornography" and (3) it was one of the largest retailers of cigarettes in the U.S.
4. Business Concern
   The company was confronted by demands for community participation and involvement to a greater extent than anticipated.
5. Providing Socially Needed Products and Services
   In attempting to combine good business with good social needs, the Committee found some new opportunities and defined some new products to meet them.
6. Fixing Responsibilities within the Organization
   The Committee found no planned effort to encourage executive participation in the communities they live in and no efforts to assess the corporation's affects on these communities.

A preliminary paper on the audit experience stated:

> The translation of these six segments into a concrete audit program is still in process. But the exploration to date has transformed the vague notion of "social responsibility" into some hard realities. This exploration also has stimulated speculation--not all of which has been self-approving or even pleasant. Indeed, the effort to date has made manifest that:
>
> a social audit reveals may more vulnerabilities than could be forseen; and
> (the company's) sales volume, costs and profits are involved in more ways and to a greater extent than had been contemplated

A second company, a bank, looked primarily to the areas of minority business and middle and low income housing. It collected cost data on hiring, out of pocket and allocated costs for training, and counted numbers of relevant personnel in the various employee grades. In its loan programs it measured costs and even attempted to determine the opportunity cost of not loaning the money elsewhere. But on determining social *benefits* of these programs the bank ran into conceptual and measurement difficulties: What activities did the loan program support? What share of these were attributable to the bank's loans? What were the activities value? Did they displace other activities; What were these values? etc.

A third company, Abt Associates, intends to include the results of its social audit in its annual report along with a Social Balance Sheet and Social Operations and Income Statement. Abt focused primarily on one constituency, the employees. Data collected included: number of minority and female managers in the firm; staff lay-offs and turn-over; judgements on people "burning out," etc. [Bauer and Fenn, 1972, p.60].

Abt described his social statements in an article dealing with the "rational management of social overhead" [Abt, 1972]. His focus is on social efficiency by which he means, "the relative costs of different equally desirable social programs, or the relative degree to which different social programs satisfy a given constituency for the same cost" [Abt, 1972, p.41].

In measuring the dollar value of benefits Abt makes the assumption that "a thing is worth what it costs or what people are willing to pay for it" and that "untried social benefits can be related to some one or more differently marketed benefits that seem similar" [Abt, 1972, p.41]. In getting at both costs and preferences for services, stratified samples are used of the employee and community populations.

The Social Financial Statements, Abt shows for a hypothetical company, contain categories on the Social Balance Sheets [Abt, 1972, p.42] such as:

SOCIAL ASSETS
  Basic Social R & D not yet applied
  Social worth of plant and equipment used for social benefit of all used thus
SOCIAL LIABILITIES
  Staff committed to non-social purposes such as money making and internal management

and on the Operating Statement [Abt, 1972, p. 43]:

SOCIAL BENEFITS
  Food services--costs and savings to staff of at-cost lunches and staff time cost
  Air Quality--cost of air conditioning
  Net promotions--no., % of total, cost in salaries and fringes
  Contributions to knowledge--no., %, $
SOCIAL COSTS
  Staff "free" time exploited no., %, $ cost, etc.

Abt states that he has committed his company of some 200 members to perform this audit and issue yearly a social balance sheet [Abt, 1971, p.47]. His concept is a challenging one and in his firm it may just work.

One final example concerns the Bank of America. Their controller stated that the problem of developing an "arithmetic of quality" (as their president calls it) has turned out to be formidable. They set out to draw up a social budget, the first step of which was to inventory "all outlays likely to be classified as social or less than fully economic."

Then they found the cost figures fuzzy, for not only did they attempt to determine the banks contribution, but they begin to calculate opportunity costs of making loans at less than full rate or the profits on the business an executive might have brought in had he not been working on a social benefit project [Andrews, 1971 (a), p.1].

The Bank then switched to examining specific activities to see if they throw off a social benefit. "For example, when the bank writes mortgages in a given area, what happens to the neighborhood? Do they affect the economy or stabilize the area? This involves evaluating social and economic trends in the area and the bank is now revising its computer system to permit such analyses. The bank has found "the 'arithmetic of quality' an elusive concept" [Andrews, 1971a]. Yet they and others persist and Bank of America's controller predicts that within three to five years annual reports will be required to include data on a company's social outlays.

The above examples of social audit reveal wide differences in scope, intent, and performance. Some phases of the studies involved an inventory of socially relevant activities, some a measurement of the resources used, others attempted to evaluate the results of corporate actions and one study involved imputing values to things both intangible and real. The range of the techniques being drawn upon are imposing and the results are positive. They do not yet meet the needs expressed by many for an arithmetic of quality.[15] And this is not surprising for there needs to be a period in which procedures are being sorted out, where different measures are used, modified and even discarded, where understanding develops and where an operational, if not a conceptual, framework emerges. The history of financial measurement has not been smooth, nor is it even ended. There is no reason for social measurement to fare any better. A start has been made and the accounting discipline can contribute to its continuation. Let us first examine the problem in more detail and then some research steps that might be taken.

SOCIAL AUDITING

NATURE OF SOCIAL MEASUREMENT

Social Audits, or any attempt at measuring social performance in an organization, can be done at a number of levels depending on the purpose and state of the measurement methodology. The basic level of measurement consists of determining the set of activities that are socially relevant, taking an *inventory*. This level of study addresses the question "What are we doing?" and identifies the universe of activities for possible further measurement.

The second, or *input* level, involves determining the categories and extent of the efforts being expended in each of the identified, socially relevant activities. This level of study addresses the question "How much are we doing?" in terms of resources and actions taken. Examples are dollars of contribution, number of man hours of released time, amount spent on minority hiring and/or training, total dollars loaned to ghetto residents or spent on constructing low income housing, etc. Two more sophisticated variants of input level measurement exist. The first calculates all the inputs in terms of common measure, "cost to the organization." This involves, as we shall see later, a number of accounting questions. A second variant is the determination of norms or standards against which the level of the firm's inputs can be compared--"Is 4% for the community enough?" It should be noted that such standards implicitly assume a common measuring technique.

The third level of measurement I will call *process* for what is examined is the transformation of the inputs into outputs. The process of course is not what is measured, although it can be evaluated as to its workings, but the immediate outputs are identified and enumerated. Thus the level of measurement counts what is immediately done or produced, e.g. the number of loans granted, number of employees trained, tons of water filtered, tons of a particular residue captured in precipitators, etc. Norms or standards are also appropriate for such "immediate products" and costs may be calculated for the process and hence attributed to the process's products--cost per loan, dollars per bottle reclaimed, etc. What is not done at this level of measurement is to make an evaluation of the "worth" of the output; this is another, higher level of measurement.

The fourth level of measurement evaluates the worth of the output, the *results*. This involves both an identification of what is being accomplished and an evaluation of the worth the accomplishment has for society. This is more than an enumeration of the immediate results and can involve second order effects, foregone alternatives, and displaced activities. Consider the example of the reclaimation of glass bottles. The value to society is not the number of bottles reclaimed nor even the cost of new bottles that are now not needed but it includes the costs that would have been incurred in cleaning up and disposing of the bottles had they not been reclaimed--or alternatively, the cost in environmental degradation the discarded bottles would have produced.

The social audits cited in the previous section operated on all of these levels. The vending machine corporation inventoried its actions and, in one or two instances, computed the resources it committed (levels one and two). The bank on the other hand attempted to measure not only the inputs and the immediate process outputs but attempted to measure the social value of its loan activities--with reportedly unsatisfactory results. Abt Associates propose to measure both the social inputs of its activities and the social results [Abt, 1972] but how successful it will be remains to be determined. The Bank of America [Andrews, 1971a] first tried to identify its socially related activities and the cost of the resources they required and ran aground on determining opportunity cost.[16] They then turned towards an inventory of results, and presumably their value, but indicated that this approach needed substantial further work.

Most of the cries for social measurement either explicitly or implicitly call for a measurement of the value of the social results. There is no question that such a measurement system would be of tremendous value. There is a question, however, if it can be developed to any extent in the near future. Nonetheless, it is important enough to warrant serious research.

The lack of such a measurement scheme does not mean the end of social audits.[17] Social needs are still present and social actions must be taken. Research directed towards improving the information on which social decisions are based is still required. One such research approach is the subject of the next section.

A RESEARCH STRATEGY

The most important information in making socially relevant decisions is the value of the resulting action. Too often, as we have discussed, determining the value of the results is difficult, involving as it does second order effects, etc. In addition, decisions must often be taken in a time frame which is too short to permit determination and evaluation of ultimate outcomes. In such cases, information must be based on something less than that optimally desired.

In many such situations the decision-maker turns to an examination of the inputs and to a judgement about the processes intended to produce the desired results. This also is the strategy adopted by accountants in conducting management or operational evaluations and in doing aspects of financial audits. Thus it would seem that where it is not possible to adequately validate the output, it is advisable to validate the process by which the output is produced to see what assumptions are being made, what variables are being considered, what alternatives are being evaluated, what decision rules are being used, and what resources are being employed. Let me refer to such a study as a process audit. I believe it is an important area for research.

Cost Measurement

A second area for research, and one that might well precede a study of process audits, involves social cost measurement. As we have seen, some social audits have gone astray through the mixing of incurred and opportunity costs. Cost attribution to social activities seem to involve three considerations:

1. Opportunity costs are particularly relevant for decision-making as they describe the cost of achieving the same ends by different means and/or the cost of using the same resource to different ends. They are very difficult to measure directly because they necessitate consideration of what "might have been." This difficulty is compounded when one also desires to aggregate these costs. Focusing on opportunity costs, except in particular situations where they can be used as standards for actual cost comparisons, can lead to a morass of computation and to inconclusive results. Even in the determination of the economic profit and loss of business entities, alternative costs are rarely, if even, used. This is not because accountants fail to recognize their value, but because over the years they have recognized the problems associated with their use.

2. Incurred costs have two main aspects:

A. Costs directly attributable to the activities-resources under consideration.

B. Costs jointly allocatable to this activity-resource and to others.

Direct costs are by definition easily identifiable once the activity-resource and its metric have been isolated. Joint costs, however, are separable, if at all, only by arbitrary decision rules. It is here that uniform and reasonably acceptable methodology needs to be developed.

3. While the identification of incurred cost involves little conceptual difficulty, their ascertainment in practice is a major problem since the activities about which the costs are being collected were not those designed to be isolated by most information processing systems. Thus a framework needs to be developed for identifying these activities and to assign to them a truly meaningful "cost."

A colleague, John Shank, and I have begun a cost measurement study which would encompass the following steps:

1. Identify through field studies in at least three business

organizations a set of socially-relevant activities and the resources which these activities use.

2. Develop criteria for deciding which of these candidates are representative of the types of problems involved in cost determination.

3. Develop the relevant metric for describing the resources committed to each activity.

4. Using these metrics, assign a "cost" to each resource used by the activities chosen.

5. Develop a generalized methodology for accomplishing this cost assignment in a manner which permits use within and among organizations.

The ultimate aim of the research is to develop a measuring methodology which will: (1) enable firms to capture relevant social costs through the regular information processing systems in a way that can be used for internal decision-making; (2) permit the public disclosure of the level of the firm's resource commitment so that comparisons can be made within and between organizations; and (3) produce an understanding of alternate methods of cost determination so that publicly disclosed data can be evaluated critically.

Process Audits

The research study of ultimate interest to me involves process audits. Such research would build upon the results of the cost measurement study and

1. characterize the social decision processes or sets of processes that have common structures

2. develop a methodology for evaluating the general quality and appropriateness of these processes

3. construct procedures by which these evaluations can be validated, disclosed, and compared between activities and between organizations.

The basic methodology would involve field work in several companies and draw heavily on the operational and financial auditing literature developed by internal auditors and certified public accountants.[18]

The immediate purpose of this research would be aimed at improving management's ability to make better socially responsible decisions as a good understanding of process can be a better guide to action than indeterminable results.

A second goal of the research is of longer range. Observation of practice as well as more formal research [Churchill, et. al., 1964] indicates that where measures are made and actions evaluated, behavior is effected. If a social auditing methodology is developed that is realistic and generally applicable in the business environment, then appropriately socially responsive decisions *will* be made. And that, in essence, is what the shouting is all about.

NOTES

[1]One writer describes as cause "a closing of the gap between people's aspirations and expectations and a recent widening of the gap between these expectations and their achievement" [Gans, 1972, p. 16]. The National Goals Research Staff in contrasting quality and economic quantity cites three major causes of concern:

1. The changing values and a rising level of our expectations concerning the goals that we should set for ourselves in both resolving inequities and improving the quality of our lives.

2. A realization that our resources, although substantial and likely to grow in a generally predictable fashion, are limited, and therefore, more consideration should be given to the setting of priorities for their use.

3. The development of a wide range of management and planning tools that offer some promise for more rational setting or priorities and for effective action" [NGRS, 1969, p. 32].

They also put forth two "additional circumstances":

1. Actions taken must be "Persuasive to citizens who are demanding a more direct representation in decisions affecting their lives."

2. Management models and society itself have "become increasingly complex and interrelated."

[2]Quoted in "American Corporations Under Fire," [1971, p. 83].

[3]Mr. Clausen, President of the Bank of America, wrote, "We need a social cost budget as well as the conventional economic cost budget. A beginning might be to ask company accountants to attempt detailed cost estimates of what management considers its major social responsibilities. How successful this will be is yet to be established but certainly some estimates are better than none. They enable companies to make better business judgements and thereby avoid abrupt changes in consequential programs. I call upon the accounting profession to help all of us work out this new arithmetic tool" [Clausen, 1971, p. 13].

One social scientist commented in this vein that "some types of progress are the logical domain of particular disciplines. Other types of progress, needed but not well implemented, are limited by the intractability of the problems to the disciplines addressing them. Social measurement is such a case and the accountants should become involved."

[5]For a well written discussion of this see Andrews [1971 (b)].

[6]See [Bauer 1966] and the [Ruggeles 1971] for early and late views on the topic.

[7]A good bibliography on the social indicator field with a brief review of the "movement" was published in January, 1971 by sociologists at Iowa State [Beal, et.al., 1971] with another planned this year.

[8]Social scientists such as Bertram Gross in [Bauer, 1966] and the National Goals Research Staff [NGRS, 1970] and businessmen such as William Stolk, Chairman of the Board of the Council for Economic Development, [Walton, 1970, pp. 66-73], Eli Goldston, President of Eastern Gas and Fuel Associates, Boston [Management Advisor, 1972, pp. 6-7] and A. W. Clausen, President of the Bank of America [Clausen, 1971].

[9]See [Sheldon and Freeman 1970], [Sheldon 1971], and [Land 1971]. For a different approach to the problem using microdata bases see [Ruggeles 1971].

[10]For a summary of the state of social reporting see [Sheldon 1971].

[11]See the dissenting notes, particularly Mr. Sporn's, in the CED's Statement on Corporate Responsibility [1971, pp. 62-74].

[12]"The supply-and-demand mechanism of the market does not make its adjustments nor allocate resources with full information about all costs that are in reality being incurred by society" [NGRS, 1970, p. 69]. See also [Beams and Fertig 1971, p. 38] with a suggestion for "pollution costs" and [Polk 1971] who estimates that the cost of getting a ton of physical resources (exclusive of stone, gravel, and other construction materials) is $260 a ton and that the cost of recycling it is probably the same.

[13]Andrews quotes an environmentalist who states, "the leaders of industry aren't evil men. Rather they work within a system where their

performance is judged by the corporate profit and loss statement which doesn't allow for social considerations" [1971 (a), p. 1].

[14]Counter arguments on pollution are not hard to find. See [Beams and Fertig, 1971, p. 39].

[15]"Most important, the development of improved social indicators and measurement techniques would aid management in finding the most appropriate corporate role in social improvement (balancing the interests of various constituencies and claimants), determining the correct strategy, evaluating the results, and justifying its actions to its constituencies. At present, many businessmen and economists are hesitant about corporations moving into social activities because neither social requirements nor corporate capabilities, actions, and results can be quantified with the exactness of commercial activities. Correspondingly, corporate constituencies and the larger society lack adequate means for judging what the corporation is really accomplishing in efforts to improve its environment" [CED, 1970, p. 48].

[16]It could be asked why they thought they could use opportunity costs in measuring social activities when we have never been able to successfully use opportunity costs in measuring financial activities on any large scale.

[17]Bauer and Penn [1972, pp. 89-125] give four reasons for a corporation to make an audit of its social activities: (1) to satisfy the conscience of corporate officers, (2) to anticipate and avoid community, government and other pressures, (3) to really solve social problems, and (4) to increase long term profits. The first requires merely an inventory and some norms, the second input and process information, the third needs these and some general feelings about the value of the results, and the fourth all categories of information.

[18]An extension of the attest function into the social area was proposed by an accountant with Price Waterhouse who is actively involved in financial audits of federal poverty programs. What he proposed is an attestation to the reasonableness of a work load analysis of federal poverty programs--a process audit [Limbert, 1971].

BIBLIOGRAPHY

Abt, Clark, "Managing to Save Money by Doing Good," *Innovation*, No. 27, 1972, pp. 38-47.

American Academy of Arts and Sciences, "Toward the Year 2000: Work in Progress," *Daedalus*, Summer 1967.

"The American Corporation under Fire," *Newsweek*, May 24, 1971, pp. 74-85.

Andrews, Fredrick, "Changing Times: Puzzled Businessmen Ponder New Methods of Measuring Success," The Wall Street Journal, December 9, 1971(a), p. 1 ff.

Andrews, Fredrick, "Changing Times: Government Statistics Are Termed Misleading as Gauges of Society," The Wall Street Journal, December 16, 1971(b), p. 1 ff.

Bauer, Raymond A. (ed.), *Social Indicators*, The MIT Press, Cambridge, Mass., 1966.

Bauer, Raymond A., and Fenn, Dan H., Jr., "The Corporate Social Audit," (Draft to be published in *Social Science Pioneer Papers*) Russell Sage Foundation, New York.

Beal, George M., et. al., *Social Indicators: Bibliography I*, Sociology Report No. 92, Iowa State University; 1971.

Beams, Floyd A. and Fertig, Paul E., "Pollution Control Through Social Cost Conversion," *Journal of Accountancy*, November 1971, pp. 37-42.

Bragdon, Joseph H. Jr. and Merlin, John A. T., "Is Pollution Profitable?", unpublished paper, Boston, 1971.

Burton, G. Malkiel and Quandt, Richard E., "Moral Issues in Investment Policy," *Harvard Business Review*, Vol. 49, No. 2, March-April 1971, pp. 37-47.

Clausen, A. W., "Toward an Arithmetic of Quality," *The Conference Board Record*, May 1971, pp. 9-13.

Churchill, Neil C., Cooper, W. W., and Sainsbury, T., "Laboratory and Field Studies of the Behavioral Effects of Audits," in Bonini, C. P., Jaedicke, R. K., and Wagner, H. M., *Management Controls*, McGraw Hill, 1964, pp. 253-267.

Committee for Economic Development, *Social Responsibilities of Business Corporations*, New York, 1971.

Council on Economic Priorities, *Efficiency in Death*, Harper and Row, New York, 1970.

Gans, Herbert J., "The American Malaise," *New York Times Magazine*, February 6, 1972, pp. 16 ff.

Land, Kenneth G., "On the Definition of Social Indicators," *The American Sociologist*, November 1971, pp. 322-325.

Limbert, G. Christian, Jr., "Evaluating Federal Poverty Programs," *Price Waterhouse Review*, Summer/Autumn, 1971, pp. 51-59.

Linowes, David F., "Social Responsibility of the Profession, *The Journal of Accountancy*, January, 1971, pp. 66-69.

National Goals Research Staff, *Toward Balanced Growth: Quantity with Quality*, U.S. Government Printing Office, July 4, 1970.

Polk, Judd, "Social Costs of Economic Growth," *The Vienna Papers*, International Chamber of Commerce, Meeting 23, pp. 31-38.

Ross, Gerald H. B., "Social Accounting: Measuring the Unmeasurable," *Canadian Chartered Accountant*, July 1971, pp. 46-54.

Ruggles, Nancy and Richard, "A Proposal for a System of Social Accounts," (paper) National Bureau of Economic Research, New York, 1971.

Sheldon, Eleanor Bernert and Moore, Wilbert E.,(eds.), *Indicators of Social Change*, Russell Sage Foundation, New York, 1968.

Sheldon, Eleanor Bernert and Freeman, Howard E., "Notes on Social Indicators: Premises and Potential," *Policy Sciences 1*, 1970, pp. 97-111.

Sheldon, Eleanor Bernert, "Social Reporting for the 1970's," in *Federal Statistics: Report of the President's Commission*, Vol. II, 1971, pp. 403-435.

U. S. Department of Health, Education, and Welfare, *Towards a Social Report*, U.S. Government Printing Office, 1969.

Managerial Accounting and Organizational Coordination

INTRODUCTION

Managerial accounting is importantly concerned with the planning and performance evaluation of the subunits of organizations (e.g., cost and profit centers, service departments, and so on). In addition, there is considerable emphasis on the co-ordination of subunit plans and performance in relation to the total organization.

Organization theory also gives much attention to the relations between organizational parts and the whole. Despite this common focus on both the accounting and the organization theory literature, there has been little attempt to collate them.

Since managerial accounting has not yet built up a cohesive foundation of principles, progress towards the development of a body of knowledge is much needed, and one path towards its development is the incorporation of theory from related areas, such as organizational behavior.

"Behavioral accountants" are in a position to help integrate knowledge from the behavioral sciences into accounting. As Lawler (1972) puts it, "should behavioral accounting researchers ensconce themselves in a well-stacked library or an ill-equipped laboratory? From my perspective it looks very much like they are going to need to do both." A similar view is expressed by Golembiewski (1972): "behavioral research in accountancy will have major characteristics of an applied science, especially early in its development . . . behavioral research in accountancy no doubt will rely heavily on theoretical constructs and measuring instruments derived from existing work."

The purpose of the present paper is to explore and collate some accounting and organization theory views of organizational coordination, or the linking of effort between organizational subunits and their relations to the total organization. The term "co-ordination" is sometimes referred to as integration in organization theory. Our attempt is to prematurely try to resolve the problems of this large and complex area, but rather to raise questions of importance and to suggest promising avenues for future research.

THE IMPORTANCE OF SUBUNITS IN ACCOUNTING AND IN ORGANIZATION THEORY

Much of the activity of management accounting deals with subunits of the organization. Comparing financial accounting with management accounting, Anthony (1965: 105) points out that financial accounting focuses on the *whole* enterprise, while management accounting is concerned more with the *parts*. The financial statements report on the overall status and performance of the organization, but management accounting reports have mostly to do with departments, products, or other subunits of the total entity. Caplan (1971: 37-38) also emphasizes that management accountants tend to deal with subunit performance.

Similarly, organization theory also pays important attention to subunits. In particular, many organization theorists have long concentrated on questions of organization *structure*, which comprises the design of and the relationships among subunits (Kast and Rosenzweig, 1970: 170-207; Filley and House, 1969: 69-100). Several of these questions have strong implications for managerial accounting. We begin with the organization theory phenomenon known as "differentiation".

DIFFERENTIATION IN THE ORGANIZATION SYSTEM

ENVIRONMENTAL INFLUENCES

Organizations are always located within larger systems of activity. Some parts of the organization, therefore, must adjust to environmental constraints and contingencies not controlled by the organization--to what economists call "exogenous variables" (Thompson, 1967: 66-67).

In comparing two Norwegian firms, Dill (1958) distinguished between environments which were relatively homogenous or heterogenous. His Alpha firm faced a relatively homogenous environment in the sense that most of its customers ordered all four product lines about twice a year and at approximately the same time of year. The firm dealt with only one labor union, and virtually all of the external groups with which it had transactions were Norwegian. Contrastingly, his Beta firm dealt in a variety of quite distinct markets, negotiated with three unions, and engaged in significant international trade, thus facing a set of relatively heterogenous environmental conditions.

Also, Dill distinguished a stable from a rapidly-shifting environment. For example, Alpha's market had not changed much in fifth years either with respect to products or to means of distribution. Beta's markets, however, had changed by growth in certain areas and disappearance in others. Eleven of the thirteen major work activities were recent, arising from expansion and diversification of customers, from rapid technological progress in the equipment and processing techniques used by Beta, and from increases in the real disposable income of Norwegian consumers.

Thompson (1967: 70-78) shows how both these dimensions of environment critically affect organizational structure. His propositions are summarized as follows. Organizations whose environments are relatively stable and homogenous will tend to be relatively simple in the structure of their boundary-spanning[1] subunits. There would be few functional divisions and, if these were subdivided, it would be into several similar sections. This organization would operate primarily through standardized rules, the departments would be rule-applying agencies, and management would consist largely of rule enforcement.

For a stable but heterogenous environment, a variety of functional divisions would be anticipated, each corresponding to a relatively homogenous environmental segment and relying primarily on standardized operating rules. Subdivision of these functional divisions would probably be by geographic or similar lines, into uniform sections, each a rule-applying agency.

When the environment becomes shifting rather than stable, standardized rules are inadequate, and cues must be taken from the environment: pre-established standardized rules tend to be supplanted, to the extent necessary, by feedback and mutual adjustment (March and Simon, 1958: 158-169). With a relatively homogenous environment, the boundary-spanning subunits need to be subdivided only to the extent that their ability to monitor the environment is overtaxed. Expectedly, subunits could be geographically segmented. But, unlike the previous cases, they would be less concerned with application of rules than with planning and adjusting to feedback of environmental changes. Regional divisions would tend to be decentralized.

With an environment both heterogenous and shifting in nature, the prediction is for boundary-spanning units to be differentiated functionally in relation to environmental segments, and to be decentralized in order to respond to fluctuations in individual sections of the environment.

In summary, we would expect variations in the two environmental variables to be reflected in the differentiation of boundary-spanning subunits. This differentiation tends to occur with respect to the relative reliance on rules versus feedback and the degree of decentralization in operation. Thompson notes that size alone does not add complexity to organization. He cites Chandler (1962), who found that copper companies, although very large as a rule, were among the least complex organizations in his study, because they produced few types of products for a well-defined market and employed routined technical operations. By contrast, hospitals and universities tend to be among the most complex of organizations, although relatively small by any measure of size.

The segmentation of subunits is made difficult when there is interdependence between segments. March and Simon (1958: 159) " . . . predict that process specialization will be carried furthest in stable environments, and that under rapidly changing circumstances specialization will be sacrificed to secure greater self-containment of separate programs." This seems consistent with Thompson's proposition that when major organizational segments are interdependent, they will be arranged into self-sufficient clusters. In business organizations such clusters are often called decentralized divisions or profit centers. The supporting argument for this proposition is that boundary-spanning units confronting heterogenous and shifting environments have serious adaptive challenges. If they are also involved in interdependencies, the resultant set of constraints and contingencies overtaxes the organization's capacity to adapt and coordinate. By diversitying into relatively independent clusters, the organization attains a manageable "bounded rationality" (Simon, 1957; Kast and Rosenzweig, 1970: 375-377).

For example, the enormous capacities of such a diversified giant as General Electric for marketing, production, etc. are not functionally arranged into organization-wide total marketing or production divisions.

Instead, there are diversified clusters, each being a profit-center division of General Electric. Chandler (1962) emphasizes though that only those large business firms supplying quite different lines of products to increasingly differentiated groups of customers have turned to the profit-center division of organization.

A major consequence of increased departmentalization and delegation of authority is increased specialization and more "local rationally" (Cyert and March, 1963: 117). This leads to a divergence of interest among organizational subunits. Individuals tend to act in furtherance of their subunit goals, with lesser regard for the organization as a whole (Dearborn and Simon, 1958). Thus, while a degree of differentiation is an organizational necessity, it inevitably creates conflict and dilemma within the organization.

TECHNOLOGICAL INFLUENCES

A number of studies, most of them fairly recent, lend support to the notion that organizational structure is to some extent dependent upon the technology used.

Earlier work by Bavelas and Leavitt used small groups (mostly consisting of five members each) to perform problem-solving tasks in laboratory settings. Communication between group members was controlled. Of most interest to our purpose is the "wheel" structure (where each "spoke" member could communicate only with the central "hub" member) and the circle (where each member can communicate with two others). The former structure can be characterized more or less as authoritarian, and the latter as decentralized. On simple, repetitive tasks the wheel was more efficient over repeated trials than the circle, although its members were less happy. However, for more complex and novel problems, more discussion of new ideas takes place in the circle, which adapts faster to solutions. The wheel tends to resist new ideas, the central member saying that he is "too busy" or that present methods are satisfactory (Leavitt, 1962). The main conclusion is that different kinds of tasks are best performed by different methods. Thus, task, technology, and structure are related.

Udy (1959) in a massive study of anthropological data on 426 nonindustrial organizations concluded that various aspects of authority, division of labor, and other variables of organization structure could be predicted as to general trend from knowledge of technology alone.

Woodward (1965) in a field study of 100 English firms found a relationship between types of technology and organization structure. The more economically successful companies in each technology group were found to have similar structural attributes. The three broad technology groups were (1) small-batch and unit production, e.g., custom electronic equipment or clothing made to order; (2) large-batch and mass production, e.g., standard industrial components and assemblies; and (3) process or continuous production, e.g., oil refining, chemicals.

Woodward's results have been questioned, and later studies are as yet inconclusive regarding the existence of a "technological imperative". Hickson, Pugh, and Phesey (1969) conclude that operations technology affects only those structural variables immediately impinged on by the workflow, but not the wider administrative structure. Mohr (1971) reviews the work on technology and structure quite thoroughly and concludes that "technology may be related to structure, but not as a magical package". Both technology and structure are complex sets of many variables, and adequate study requires precise specification, definition, and measurement of individual variables, as well as consideration of other related factors. However, the existence of--and need for--subunit differentiation, whether as a function of technology or not, are generally accepted.

DIFFERENTIATION: NATURE OF SUBUNIT DIFFERENCES

Of interest is a large field study of twenty companies (Burns and Stalker, 1961) and the relation of organization structure with success in adapting to changes in market conditions and technological progress. These researchers created two broad classifications of organizational structure, organic and mechanistic. Reminiscent of the Bavelas and Leavitt studies, they found the former to be better adapted to change and the latter to stable conditions. Characteristics of the two types have been tabulated as follows:

Index	*Organic*	*Mechanistic*
Span of Control	Wide	Narrow
Number of Levels of Authority	Few	Many
Ratio of Administrative to Production Personnel	High	Low
Range of Time Span an Employee Can Commit Resources	Long	Short
Degree of Centralization in Decision Making	Low	High
Proportion of Persons in One Unit Having Opportunity to Interact with Persons in Other Units	High	Low
Quantity of Formal Rules	Low	High
Value Orientation	External to Organization	Internal to Organization
Specificity of Job Goals	Low	High
Specificity of Required Activities	Low	High
Content of Communications	Advice and Information	Instructions and Decisions
Range of Compensation	Narrow	Wide
Range of Skill Levels	Narrow	Wide
Knowledge-based Authority	High	Low
Position-based Authority	Low	High

Source: Ralph M. Hower and Jay W. Lorsch, "Organizational Inputs", in John A. Seiler, *Systems Analysis in Organizational Behavior*. (Homewood, Ill.: Richard D. Irwin, Inc. and The Dorsey Press, 1967), p. 168.

SUBUNIT DIFFERENTIATION: SPECIFIC VARIABLES

Since the work of Lawrence and Lorsch (1967) provides an excellent framework, we will use it as the basis for this section. These researchers set up four dimensions of differentiation within organizational subunits, which are as follows:

FORMALITY OF STRUCTURE

Differences between subunits with respect to formality of structure were computed on the basis of six characteristics, namely the size of the average span of control, the number of levels to a shared superior, the time span of review of departmental performance, the specificity of review of departmental performance, the importance of formal rules, and the specificity of criteria for evaluation role occupants.

It was found[2] that production departments had the most formal structures, with basic research units being the least formally structured and sales departments having an intermediate position. The characteristic of degree of structure as a factor in subunit differentiation is not much discussed in the accounting literature. The only reference that was found was Anthony (1965: 37-41), who used this characteristic to differentiate between his concepts of the activities involved in strategic planning and management control.

Since several procedures of interest to managerial accounting are involved in the underlying variables of formality of structure (such as the time span and specificity of review of departmental performance), it is suggested that this be viewed as a promising area for future accounting research.

INTERPERSONAL ORIENTATION

Prior research had suggested that people in different subunits would tend to be more effective given different interpersonal styles related to the nature of their task. Members of departments involved in either highly certain or highly uncertain task environments would develop task-oriented interpersonal orientations. People in units with moderately uncertain tasks would develop relationship-oriented styles. The measure of this orientation was a standard pen-and-pencil test, the Fiedler Least Preferred Coworker Instrument (Fiedler, 1967).

Production engineers and other manufacturing personnel, whose tasks were relatively certain, were expected to be concerned more with getting the job done than with maintaining social relationships. Research scientists and engineers were also expected to be predisposed toward task accomplishment, the basic scientists more so than the applications engineers, but neither so much as the production personnel. Sales and marketing people, who were engaged in a moderately uncertain task, were predicted to care most about positive social interaction with their coworkers. These predictions were all generally supported by the actual data of the study.

Again, the accounting literature is extremely sparse in this area. It does seem to be important, since it is likely to impinge on relationships between accountants and managers.

TIME ORIENTATION

This was measured by asking managers, in a questionnaire, how much of their time was devoted to activities that contributed to company profits in different future time periods: one month or less; one to three months; three to twelve months; and over one year. Both production and sales department members, as one might expect, had a relatively short time orientation, often less than one month. This was consistent with the rapid feedback available from both the market and the technological-processing sectors of the environment.

Contrastingly, administrators and scientists in the fundamental research laboratories were oriented often several years into the future.

This is not unexpected, since tangible results of effort could seldom be judged before solution of scientific and technical problems leading eventually to new products or processes.

Time orientation is dealt with to some extent in the accounting literature. Usually, it is noted that the manufacturing orientation especially is typically very short (Anthony, 1965: 93; Bourque, 1970: 4-39). Also, it is often stated that the lower the level in the hierarchy, the more frequent should be the reporting cycle (e.g., Welsch, 1971: 500-511). Generally, however, there is some tendency to make reports "repetitive and relate to specific and short time spans" (Welsch, 1971: 499). Also, the different time orientation of various organization subunits is not much considered. For example, the accounting concept of "operating cycle" is seemingly always used in relation to the entire organization, rather than--as appears to be more appropriate--respective subunits which may have considerably different individual operating cycles.

GOAL ORIENTATION

Probably the most obvious aspect of subunit differentiation is the orientation of members towards goals. This is due to the fact that various subunits basically exist to deal with different parts of the environment and to perform different tasks.

To measure the subunit goal orientations, questionnaire data were collected by asking managers to indicate their degree of concern with nine different considerations arising from a new idea, three each dealing with the marke (e.g., the effect of new products resulting from the proposed idea on sales of existing products), the manufacturing process (e.g., technical problems which might result from the proposed idea), and research (e.g., the technical capability of the research staff to conduct research on the new idea). Responses turned out to be largely as expected. This is consistent with prior research supporting the hypothesis that each executive tends to perceive those aspects of a situation that relate specifically to the activities and goals of his department, and that the criteria of selection become internalized (Dearborn and Simon, 1958).

As observed before, there is a tendency in the accounting literature to emphasize cost and profit considerations, perhaps at the expense of other important criteria, in subunits (Caplan, 1971: 19). However, some accountants show awareness of this possible shortcoming. For instance, Heckert and Willson (1967: 564-565) suggest that reports should be couched in terms familiar to users, recommending that tons, man-hours, and machine operating hours are likely to mean more than dollar costs alone to manufacturing executives. Anthony (1965: 42) states that "although management control systems have financial underpinnings, it does not follow that money is the *only* basis of measurement, or even that it is the most important basis. Other quantitative measurements, such as enrollment, grades, market share, yields, productivity measures, tonnage of output, and so on, are useful. So are non-quantitative expressions of quality, ability, cooperation, and other attributes." Horngren (1967: 282) suggests that there are two conflicting tendencies: overemphasis on multiple goals may lead to diffusion of effort, while overemphasis on a single goal may lead to increased inefficiency but also to less effective over-all outcomes.[3]

At this stage it is worth reviewing the evidence we have summarized.

Based on uncertainty attributes of the organizational environment, Lawrence and Lorsch were able to predict departmental differentiation rankings with respect to four specific differentiation variables. The data supported their predictions. Of course, the findings indicate only general tendencies, and one cannot confidently predict precisely how any single organization will "fit" its environment.

These researchers went on to construct a scale of the "required" degree of differentiation with respect to each of the four variables appropriate for each department.[4] Then a measure of economic performance for each of the six organizations was constructed[5] and compared with the degree of required differentiation achieved. It was found that high economic performance was consistent with achievement of the appropriate degree of differentiation. We do not wish to make too much of this point yet, since further factors remain to be considered. However, we should note that since accounting is vitally concerned with measuring economic performance, it should therefore also be concerned with an underlying determinant of performance, namely the degree of subunit differentiation both required and actually attained. There seems to be a high priority attaching to accounting research into this topic.

THE INTEGRATION CONCEPT

As necessary background for discussing integration, we begin by reviewing very briefly the nature of differentiation. Differentiation was described as the variations in cognitive and emotional orientations between managers in different functional departments, and differences in the degree of formal structure within these departments. Complex organizations (those with more than one or two subunits) tend to segment the organization into parts, each to deal with a limited section of the environment. In the Lawrence and Lorsch (1967) research, each of the ten organizations studied dealt with a market subenvironment (the task of the sales organization), a techno-economic subenvironment (the task of the manufacturing unit), and a scientific subenvironment (the task of the research department). Within any industry, each of these subenvironments differed with respect to the relative degree of homogeneity or heterogeneity and the extent of uncertainty which it presented.

For instance, in the container industry it was found that all aspects of the environment were relatively homogenous and certain. However, in the plastics industry, there was a range from high certainty in the manufacturing segment to great uncertainty in the scientific subenvironment. Also, the entire environment was characterized as more diverse. Therefore, in the economically successful organizations in the container industry there was less differentiation than in the successful plastics organizations. Less effective organizations in both these industries were less well matched with the degree of environmental demand for differentiation.

It was expected that the less the degree of differentiation between departments, the more effective would be the degree of integration[6] between them. Consistently, the more differentiation between departments, the more difficulty they encountered in integration. This inverse relationship was confirmed by a Spearman rank-order correlation significant at the 0.05 level. However, the highest performing organizations tended to achieve greater degrees of integration with greater differentiation. This raises the question of how they were able to achieve effective integration in the face of the centrifugal forces of differentiation. We now proceed to outline the devices found to resolve this conflict.

INTEGRATION THROUGH CONFLICT RESOLUTION

It is most instructive to consider conflict resolution in the setting where it is most plainly evident and greatly important, namely the plastics industry study where the six organizations examined showed the highest degree of differentiation. In the present section, therefore, we limit ourselves accordingly.

Every organization had assigned to managers at the required level in each department the formal responsibility for integrating their department's contributions to product and process changes with those of other departments. These integrators usually had to be at the lower managerial echelons to have access to the knowledge needed to carry out the detailed activities of integration dictated by the environment.

In addition, all organizations had established departments with specific major responsibility for integrating the interactions of the basic functional departments. Also, beside the lower echelon detailed integration activities, upper level executives performed integrative roles. However, this higher-level integration dealt with the broader, issues of policies and strategy, rather than detailed, frequently-occurring decision making.

In the discussion to follow, we will use the terms "resolution of conflict" and "joint decision-making" interchangeably. It seems reasonable to do so on the basis that they relate to the same process: conflict resolution being the means of achieving the desired result of joint decision-making.

Six factors were found that distinguish between the higher-performing and lower-performing organizations in the plastics industry. These were as follows.

INTERMEDIATE POSITION OF INTEGRATORS

It was predicted and verified that the effectiveness of integrators was related to their own orientations and the structure of their departments. Integrators having goal, time, and interpersonal orientations that were intermediate compared to those of managers in the different departments being linked were more effective than if they veered too much toward one or the other orientation. Similarly, greatest effectiveness resulted from the structure of the integrating department being approximately equidistant in nature from those of the departments with higher and lower degrees of structural formality. Essentially, for integrators to span these differentiation distances, they needed to be not too unlike members of the departments being linked. However, if integrators were perceived as being too similar to one particular department or another, the others would tend to see them as overly receptive to the views and problems of the like department and not sufficiently attuned to the attitudes and needs of other departments. Therefore, the intermediate position was necessary.

INFLUENCE OF INTEGRATORS

Clearly, the degree of integrators' influence and effectiveness would be expected to be interconnected. Influence may stem from a number of sources, such as hierarchical position or being knowledgeable or possession of expertise. The research suggested that influence based on hierarchical position was insufficient for effective integrating activity. Functional managers higher in knowledge and competence felt that they had more to contribute in decision-making, and, while recognizing positional influence, would tend to resent its exercise, especially if it seemed inconsistent with the facts of the situation.

This does not dismiss hierarchical influence as unnecessary, but simply as inadequate by itself. It says that effective integrators also need influence which is seen by others to derive importantly from detailed knowledge and high competence.

REWARD SYSTEMS FOR INTEGRATORS

The third factor expected to be relevant was the extent to which integrators felt that they were evaluated and rewarded on the basis of over-all performance of the cluster of subunits within their sphere of integration. As mentioned before, all integrators had functional responsibilities as well as integrative roles. If they felt that the former area was the most important factor in the judgment of their performance, they would have less incentive to work at purely integrative tasks.

Findings were as expected. Integrators in the more effectively performing organizations seemed to be receiving signals, explicit or implicit, from their superiors that a significant part of their job was the over-all results for the products flowing jointly from subunits within their zone of responsibility. In low-performing organizations the particular incentives to work at conflict resolution were not so noticeable.

So far, we have dealt with three factors primarily affecting the integrators: intermediate personal orientation and department structure, high influence based on knowledge and competence, and incentives for conflict resolution. Each of these factors has tended to be associated with more effective organization performance. We now proceed to consider three further factors affecting not primarily the integrators only, but also managers in general and the decision processes of the organizations.

TOTAL LEVEL OF INFLUENCE

It is clear (Smith and Ari, 1964; Likert, 1961) that the total amount of influence in an organization is not a fixed amount, to be allocated and handed down from the top of the organization, as has sometimes been suggested. It has been found that the total amount of influence can increase or decrease, and that an increased amount felt by particular managers or subunits need not imply a dorresponding decrease elsewhere in the organization.

Lawrence and Lorsch (1967: 70-71) report that in the higher-performing organizations the typical manager felt, due to his knowledge and the positional authority held by him, that he had considerable influence in joint decision-making. Managers throughout all departments in lower-performing organizations generally felt themselves to have lower influence in decisions.

Two principal hypotheses for the correspondence between high felt influence and enhanced organizational effectiveness are (a) Improved motivation--if managers feel that their opinions carry weight, they are more likely to act vigorously on their portions of the participatively-produced plan, and less likely to feel alienated from the decisions taken and other departments involved. (b) Improved information--increased influence given to all decision participants is likely to elicit and give consideration to a greater total amount of information, judgment, and knowledge, thus leading to better quality decisions.

INFLUENCE LOCATED AT THE REQUISITE LEVEL

It appeared useful in the integration activity to have, within each functional department, influence located at the management level where the knowledge for decision-making was available. When managers felt that they had *both* the required influence *and* and the necessary knowledge, they expressed the most confidence at their ability to resolve conflict. The research indicated that the more effective the performance of the organization, the more congruent the levels influence and requisite knowledge were found to be.

MODES OF CONFLICT RESOLUTION

Three main modes of conflict resolution were seen:

(a) *Confrontation:* an open exchange of information, views, and differences with ability and willingness to work through these towards a solution. Confrontation tends to have the advantage of leading to well thought-out decisions and to effective resolution of conflict. However, it requires a high level of trust and mutual confidence, much interpersonal skill, and the consumption of relatively large amounts of time, intellectual effort, and emotional energy. Hence, other modes are often found in use.

(b) *Compromise:* While the attempt to smooth over differences is often appealing, and seems easy to use, it does not always solve conflict problems. The problems may not disappear with mere cordiality and the passage of time, but may worsen by being left unattended. The result can be a smoldering, spreading subsurface set of conflicts. Maybe the result is organizational inaction, with friendly but ineffective groups.

(c) *Forcing:* Another mode is the use of power (based on knowledge, position, or other factors) to wrest a one-sided decision from the struggle. This may be fact, effective, and easy to apply. However, it is open to the fairly obvious weaknesses of possibly ignoring relevant and useful knowledge, and of creating resistance by parties who feel resentful at the coercion.

The study found that generally the confrontation mode was relied on more in the higher-performing organizations. Smoothing was most prevalent in the lower performers. Also, there was a tendency for forcing to be found more in high than in low performers. This suggests the usefulness of achieving conflict resolution, even by forcing if confrontation is not effective, rather than avoiding resolution by smoothing.

Having summarized the findings with respect to conflict resolution in the six plastics industry organizations, we need to consider other environments and organizations to better understand some more general basic patterns and integration and differentiation.

INTEGRATIVE PATTERNS

The plastics organizations, given that their environments were the most heterogenous and most turbulent, tended to be more highly differentiated than the food or container organizations. This condition of very high differentiation called for powerful integrative activity. These were found to include formal integrating departments and also cross-functional teams, as well as the six devices of conflict resolution described above.

By way of contrast, the container industry environment was relatively homogenous and stable. Hence, its functional departments were not highly differentiated. The need for integration was therefore less. The only formal integrative device in use was the management hierarchy, which tended toward the mechanistic organizational model. However, this hierarchical organization met conflict with effective processes of resolution. For example, the sales and production departments, which were closely and importantly involved in cooperation on crucial issues of scheduling and delivery, both felt that they had substantial influence in these decisions. Relative to these decisions, influence was mostly located at the top of the organization. The strong influence of top managers flowed not only from their positions, but also their competence and the fact that the requisite knowledge tended to be located at this hierarchical level.

The high-performing organizations relied mainly on confrontation for conflict resolution, but while significantly less, there was also substantial smoothing and forcing. Apparently, confrontation was much used for resolution of technical and quality problems, handled at the requisite intermediate level of hierarchy. However, the substantial smoothing and forcing at the top apparently was not perceived by lower participants as the arbitrary wielding of positional power so much as decision-making by the competent and knowledgeable senior managers. The extensive use of smoothing, seemingly the back-up technique used in the high-performing organization, appeared to work as a means of maintaining good relations after the making of decisions unpopular (even if seen as not unreasonable) with a particular department. Thus, contrary to the plastics organizations, smoothing seemed to be functional in this situation. So effective conflict-resolution techniques existed in these classical models, hierarchically-structured container organizations.

Clearly, the two industries reflected very differently structured organizations, probably attractive to members likely to diverge considerably in personality traits according to whether they felt more comfortable with high independence and ambiguity or the opposite. The two represent extremes on the environmental scales of homogeneity and rate of change. In one innovation was the dominant issue; in the other it was regularity of schedules and consistent quality of output.

The food industry tended to be in between these extremes, but more like plastics than like containers. Its integrating devices were like those of the plastics firms though less elaborate, and provided linkage at the lower and middle levels of management. Also similar were the effective devices for conflict resolution. Hence, its most effective organization had, like those in the other industries, developed attributes of differentiation and integration in mutual balance and consistent with the nature of the environment. To give an over-all bird's eye view, we reproduce below a table of comparison from Lawrence and Lorsch (1967: 138).

COMPARISON OF INTEGRATIVE DEVICES IN THREE HIGH-PERFORMING ORGANIZATIONS

	Plastics	*Food*	*Container*
Degree of differentiation	10.7	8.0	5.7
Major integrative devices	(1) Integrative department	(1) Individual integrators	(1) Direct managerial contact
	(2) Permanent cross-functional teams at three levels of management	(2) Temporary cross-functional teams	(2) Managerial hierarchy
	(3) Direct managerial contact	(3) Direct managerial contact	(3) Paper system
	(4) Managerial hierarchy	(4) Managerial hierarchy	
	(5) Paper system	(5) Paper system	

*High score means greater actual differentiation

Lawrence, Paul R. and Jay W. Lorsch, *Organization and Environment* (Homewood, Ill.: Richard D. Irwin, Inc., 1969), p. 138.

TECHNIQUES OF INTEGRATION AND COORDINATION

The terms "integration" and "coordination" both appear frequently in the organization theory literature and generally are used with similar meaning. We shall treat them as synonyms.

While Lawrence and Lorsch (1967) deal with integration as a process flowing from differentiation, Thompson (1967) tends to approach coordination as arising from interdependencies. No matter whether approached from the one side or the other, however, we shall describe below a classification of coordination devices. Since they are from Thompson, the classification is built on types of interdependence.

Previously, we referred to the type of interdependence arising between subunits simply because they belong to the same organization: thus, failure of one can affect the other by endangering the entire organization, or use of scarce resources in one prevents their use in another. This is called *pooled interdependence* (Thompson, 1967: 54).

Another form of interdependence is due to serial type activities, where outputs of one subunit become the inputs of another. For example, plant Alpha produces components to be assembled in plant Beta. They both have pooled interdependence to be sure. But also, Alpha must act properly before Beta can function, and the serial nature and sequence of their relationship can be stated. We call this *sequential interdependence*, and observe that it is not symmetrical (Thompson, 1967: 54).

A third form of interdependence is *reciprocal*, where the output of each subunit so related becomes input for the other. For instance, an airline maintenance unit supplies input (a serviceable aircraft) to the operations subunit. In turn, an aircraft requiring maintenance is the output of operations as an input to maintenance. These relations have a pooled aspect of interdependence, and also a serial characteristic, since the aircraft must be used in sequence first by one, then by the other. However, the distinctive characteristic is the reciprocity, with each unit open to dependencies on the other. An example is Leontief input-output analysis, on a dynamic basis, perhaps scaled down to represent a simple, multi-unit organization.

The three types of interdependence tend to occur as follows: all organizations have pooled interdependence, and more complex ones also have sequential interdependence. The most complex have all three types. Thus, the presence of sequential interdependence indicates the presence also of pooled interdependence. The presence of reciprocal interdependence indicates that there will also be sequential and pooled interdependence.

Each type of interdependence becomes harder to coordinate: with pooled interdependence, an unexpected event may be confined to one subunit and prevented from spreading unless too great (e.g., firewalls, bulkheads, physical distance, etc.). Sequential interdependence and unexpected events may require adjustment in each subunit in the sequence (e.g., the "domino theory", seniority ladders for promotions, slippage on a "critical path" link on a construction project). With reciprocal interdependence, the unexpected contingency can affect all interacting subunits, often in complex and hard-to-predict fashion. Thus, the three types of interdependence are successively more difficult to coordinate, and thus more costly, with Thompson (1967: 55) noting that the measurement of such costs is "far from perfect", an observation of interest to accountants. Thompson states a relationship of correspondence between the types of interdependence and the types of coordination, building on work by March and Simon (1958).

With *pooled interdependence*, coordination by *standardization* is usual. This consists of the establishment of rules, or routines, which direct and constrain action by each unit into compatibility with those of other units in the interdependency relationship. It is important for the rules to be internally consistent, which requires that they apply under conditions which are relatively repetitive, stable, predictable (to match rules with needs for decisions), and simple and homogenous enough to permit facile identification of situations with the relevent rules.

For *sequential interdependence*, coordination by *plan* is accomplished by setting up schedules for the flows between subunits. Coordination by plan does not demand quite the same degree of stability and routine necessary for standardization. Therefore, it is more adaptable to changing environmental conditions.

With *reciprocal interdependence*, coordination requires the use and exchange of new information which may trigger revised action. This coordination by *mutual adjustment* may often require devices other than the formal hierarchy (see Lawrence and Lorsch, 1967: 138), and the more variable and uncertain the situation, the more reliance needs to be placed upon these means.

Since the types of interdependence grow successively more complex, and the corresponding types of coordination require successively more effort and cost, organizations attempt to departmentalize by grouping subunits so as to minimize coordination costs. Further, they try to reduce thier need for reliance on the more costly and complex coordination devices by uncertainty avoidance procedures such as negotiated environment, self-confirming plans, and cognitive limits on rationality (Cyert and March, 1968: 114-125).

ACCOUNTING VIEWS OF COORDINATION

It was stated earlier that managerial accounting was concerned mainly with measurements relating to organizational subunits. Also, however, it is concerned with the integration of these measures relating both to subunit clusters and to the total organization. This concern for integration is manifested in a number of ways. One aspect is the preparation of consolidated financial statements, for reflecting the aggregate accounting measures of larger groupings, up to and including the total organization. Techniques to facilitate the preparation of consolidated financial statements are given in Copeland (1970: 23-55), who suggests the following.

The use of a parallel classification of accounts by all member companies aids the consolidation procedure. Standardized charts of accounts, methods of accounting, and form of presentation of results should be used by all affiliated companies. Also, all related companies should observe the same fisacl year so far as possible, and should arrange for consistent deadlines and speedy transmission of data for consolidation purpsoes. These latter points are especially important when there is need for the interfacing of computer systems for multi-unit organizations. Copeland also discusses uniform procedures for dealing with intercompany transactions, the separation of minority interest equities, the distinction between pre-acquisition and post-acquisition retained earnings, and so on. Generally, it seems that the matters relating to the integrative process of consolidation of accounts fall mainly under Thompson's category of pooled interdependence and coordination by standardization, with also some degree of sequential interdependence and coordination by scheduling.

Uniform accounting systems are sometimes instituted by groups of organizations in order to achieve proper comparisons of organizational performance against that of measures of the group tendency or of reference organizations. Examples are the uniform classification and reporting systems and the resultant aggregate industry-wide comprehensive reports of the National Retail Association, the American Hospital Association, and the Edison Electric Institute.

Turning to another facet of accounting coordination, namely the budgeting process, we may note that Heckert and Willson (1967: 16-17) describe coordination as one objective of budgeting. In fact, they state that in some respects this is the most important purpose of budgeting. It is accomplished by means of gearing the level and timing of activities to the expected general trend of business conditions, by allocating resources (especially equipment, inventories, and funds) to ensure proper matching of related input-output exchanges, and to avoid bottlenecks by balancing the capacities and levels of activity of respective facilities and the functional processes (sales, production, etc.).

Bourque (1970: 4-8) notes the coordination aspect of budgeting with respect to flows down the hierarchy of top management forecasts of expected economic conditions, objectives, and resources available, followed by flows up the hierarchy of subunit budgets. These are checked for mutual consistency and then aggregated to be checked for the degree to which they fulfill top management's objectives and resource availabilities. More than one iteration and series of adjustments may be required to obtain the desired degrees of mutual consistency and aggregate satisfactoriness.

Horngren (1967: 122) states that "Budgets help management to coordinate as follows: 1. The existence of a well-laid plan is the major step toward achieving coordination. Executives are forced to think of the relationship of individual operations, other operations, and the company as a whole. 2. Budgets help to restrain the empire-building efforts of executives. Budgets broaden individual thinking by helping to remove unconscious biases on the part of engineering, sales, and production officers. 3. Budgets help to search out weaknesses in the organizational structure. The administration of budgets isolates problems of communication, of fixing responsibility, and of working relationships."

Welsch (1971: 84) provides a diagram illustrating the composition of the annual budget. This diagram is illustrated on the following page.

These illustrations from the accounting literature seem consistent with the concepts of integration, the nature of interdependencies, and the techniques of coordination which Lawrence and Lorsch (1967) and Thompson (1967) suggest. It is apparent that accounting processes play a major part in the coordination activity. A useful and very clearly written overview of this is given in Anthony (1971). We now will attempt to show more generally some of the relations between coordination and managerial accounting procedures.

ACCOUNTING IN THE COORDINATION PROCESS

We previously discussed the use of standardized operating procedures as one means of coordinating activities. Those procedures tend to change slowly, to give stability to the organization, and to influence (often to a large degree) the decisions made in the organization. Now we will consider some important features of standard operating procedures that appear to be major in nature as related with a number of prominent accounting processes. Cyert and March (1963: 102-113) discuss standard operating procedures within the framework of general choice procedures, which are characterized by: (a) *Uncertainty avoidance*--whereby firms adopt practices that minimize the need for predicting uncertain future events. One method of so doing is the establishment and enforcement of standardized decision rules. (b) *Maintaining the rules*--so that once established the rules are abandoned only reluctantly and under duress. The difficulties of modifying a system as complex as a large modern firm make managers cautious about change. (c) *Use simple rules*--where firms rely on individual "judgment" to allow flexibility around simple rules. Frequently, a decision rule comprises a simple procedure and an accompanying set conditions (perhaps not overly precise) under which it may be modified.

Four major types of specific operating procedures are considered below. They are as follows.

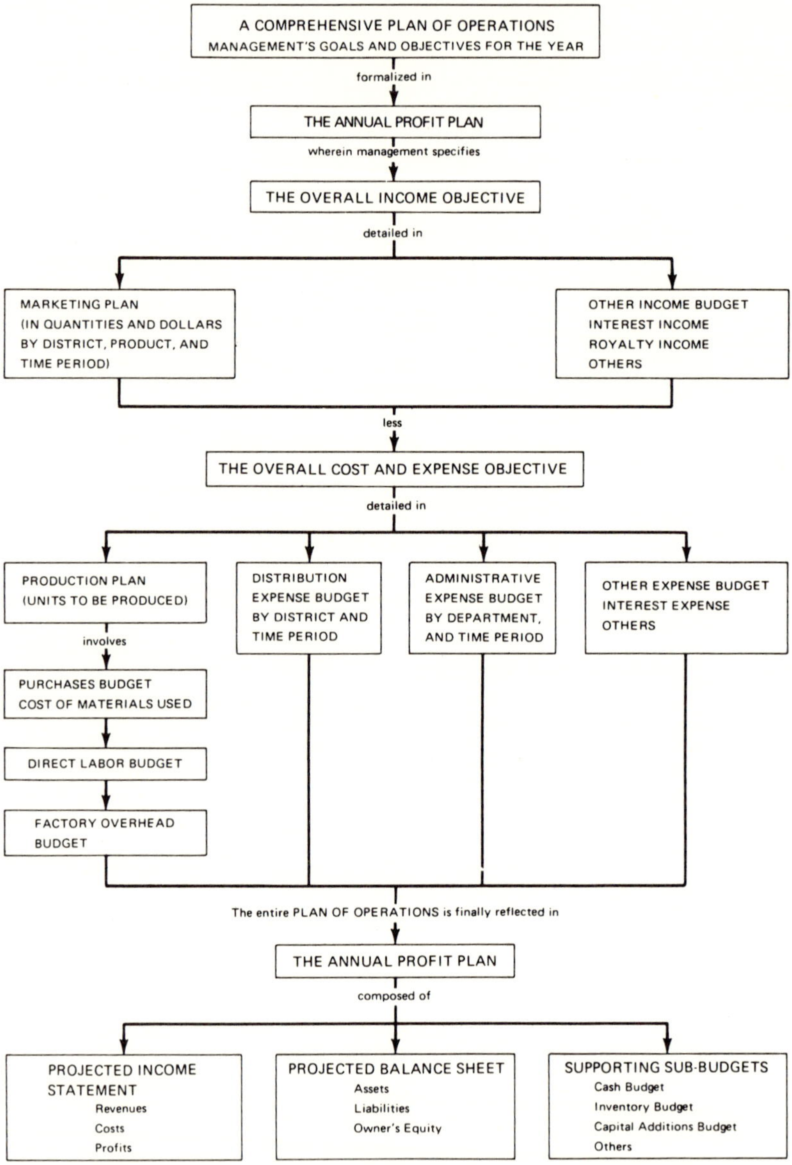

ILLUSTRATION 7 / THE ANNUAL PROFIT PLAN—ITS DEVELOPMENT AND COMPOSITION

TASK PERFORMANCE RULES--These rules govern how component XYZ is to be fabricated, or how the books are kept. Examples of the latter are the strong recommendations in favor of maintaining budget manuals (see Welsch, 1971: 79) and systems or procedures manuals (see Bourque, 1970: 4-17). Cyert and March point out that:

> "When a business firm hires an accountant . . . it hires not only an individual but also a large number of standard operating procedures that have been trained into the new member of the organization by outside agencies. One of the important consequences of professionalization in general is that extra-organizational groups have the responsibility of providing task performance rules for the organization.
>
> "The rules of good business practice . . . have a similar effect. Enforced by management literature, management consultants, accounting firms, . . . 'good practice' . . . tends to be shared among firms . . . It is clear that they serve the important function of providing an operational procedure for the manager to use in a situation of comparative ambiguity. Insofar as the external situation consists in other firms, it becomes predictable . . . in the areas covered by standard practice. Insofar as potential failure is of concern to the decision-maker, 'standardization' provides a defense."

Of course, the above refers not only to accounting, but clearly the accounting elements are not insignificant.

RECORDS AND REPORTS--These are kept on a permanent, continuing basis by just about every organization. These constitute a "major component of standard operating procedures. Just as we could describe an organization in terms of the task specifications it made, we can also describe it by the kinds of records and reports it maintains over time." (Cyert and March, 1963: 106). They go on to note that records such as financial statements are standard cost reports have short run effect on control merely because they are kept, and organization members presume that they are kept for a purpose or, conversely, that their existence will bring about some purpose of them.

Also, records are needed to help the firm predict its environment. Since predictions tend to be based on simple assumed relations between past and future, records of the past and of relations between events over time become necessary. Two important consequences of this dependence on records for predictive purposes are: firstly, the significance of records for members of the organization is high (for instance, allocation of resources to various subunits may depend greatly on rough estimates of future events) and the past record (thus, there is pressure for individuals to "look good" on the record); secondly, the nature of the records kept will determine in large measure what aspects of the environment will be observed, and thus affect the character of the decisions which get made. Cyert and March observe that this induces more stability over time of organizational decisions than if there were no (or fewer) records of prior experience. However, while making for more effective handling of previously-experienced situations, they also normally tend to retard adjustment to strikingly different situations. Here we see another type of coordination at work, namely the consistent matching of past and future decisions.

INFORMATION-HANDLING RULES--Information-handling rules are required in any large-scale organization for reasonable assurance that desired information will be available when and where it is wanted. Hence, a communication system is specified in the routine operational procedures of the organization. Cyert and March (1963: 109-110) discuss two aspects of standard operating procedure relative to information-handling: *routing* rules and *filtering* rules. *Routing* rules specify what constitutes "through channels" communication. Often the standard organization chart is accepted as the map of authorized "channels". The reason for extensive use of "channels" routing rules for information flow is that organizations attempt to create subunits in such a way that there is minimal dependence between them. The aim is that each can ignore the other except for an irreducible number of special decisions. "Since information needs and task specialization are highly correlated, it is appropriate to process information through the hierarchy defined in terms of task specialization. The rules themselves also serve to accentuate the specialization; for example, they make it relatively awkward to maintain a continuing close connection between production decisions and sales strategy decisions" (Cyert and March, 1963: 109). Thus, we see here an instance of information routing related with the degree of differentiation in an organization.

An important feature of routing rules is their relation with *filtering* at the various communication relay points. Cyert and March (1963: 110) point out that biases tend to enter into the filtering process. They maintain, and support with persuasive evidence, the propensities of sales departments to have consistent biases with respect to sales estimates, of accounting departments to filter cost data differently from other departments, and so on. They also note, however, that organizations learn to expect and discount these biases, although it is not clear how long and how efficient this learning process may be under various conditions. Nonetheless, it is an integrative tnedency which counteracts the "differentiation" of information with departmental bias.

In the long run, one method of adjusting to unreliability of information is to develop decision procedures which do not take into account apparently relevant information. This tendency of biased internal filtering, plus the pressure of external uncertainty encourage the use of decision procedures that do not require more than the simplest, most easily verifiable information. Again, the direction is towards coordination through attempted avoidance of differential departmental filtering of information.

At times, information is condensed and summarized as it traverses the organization, and some information never reaches certain points. The existence of such dead ends in information leads to decision-making that employs heavy reliance upon contingencies: decisions are used as devices for learning about their unanticipated consequences through outcries or other quick feedback. "Simulation in the raw" is the term used for this strategy (Cyert and March, 1963: 110). We note here use of another integrative device, namely the use of feedback or, in Thompson's terminology, mutual adjustment.

PLANNING generally involves the allocation of resources among the various alternative activities open to the organization and its subunits. It ranges from short-run operating budgeting to long-run planning of capital expenditures. Cyert and March suggest that long-term planning plays a relatively minor role in the firm.[7] However, business firms do enter into activities describable as, and frequently entitled, "planning". Such planning activities are normally as routinized as other standard operating procedures and follow a fixed time cycle. As an example, Cyert and March offer the budget (Cyert and March, 1963: 110-112). Two basic roles in a modern large-scale corporation are assigned to the budget.

For one thing, it serves as a management control device to implement plans that have been adopted and to check actual operating results against those of the plan. The other aspect employs the budget as a device to establish feasible programs. In either event, the budget tends to reflect, ahead of time, a set of firmly-made commitments and a set of firmly-held expectations. Although they may contain flexible parts, budgets importantly specify the framework within which the firm intends to operate and to assess its degree of achievement. The following four generalizations on plans are set forth:

i. A plan is a goal.--Under uncertainty, predictions are not necessarily realized. Planning functions not only to predict, but as a set of organizational goals. Within limits, and varying according to circumstances, behavior can be induced towards fulfillment of stated goals.

ii. A plan is a schedule.--It sets out not only goals, but intermediate stages along the way to goal accomplishment. These stages are broken down by segments of time, stating for each an acceptable level of achievement. It interrelates the over-all aspirations for the total organization with a set of decomposed subplans, consistent with the entire "master" plans.

Consistency is the essential feature of coordination by scheduling. In the budget process, the sum of the parts must equal the whole, and the individual parts must be synchronized to mutual compatibility. For example, it is usual to follow an iterative process in the budget cycle whereby the desired aggregate budget figures of top management and the sum of the provisional subunit budget figures are adjusted to conform with each other. This may require numerous iterations. Moreover, mutual consistency is required between long-range and short-range budgets, between cash, working capital, and operating budgets, and between all of these and the capital expenditure budget.

There is also need to ensure that the basic common assumptions underlying the budget are consistent throughout the organization: for example, if the sales department was to budget on a significantly different forecast of sales volume than the manufacturing department, this would almost inevitably cause inventory over-accumulations or shortages, undesired fluctuations in production scheduling and lot sizes, missed sales opportunities or costly markdowns, undesired layoffs or large overtime expense, and so on.

Most of the coordination responsibility involved is the task of the central budget officer and his staff, i.e., it is an *accounting* function (Heckert and Willson, 1967: 20-32). It is more important for all organization subunits to share the same basic budget assumptions to be the best possible in predictive value. Inconsistency involves the potential of bottlenecks, serious intra-organizational conflict, and desperate "fire-fighting" measures, whereas inaccuracy (if shared) is probably more easily coped with by simple "across the board" adjustments (which are in any event almost sure to be necessary anyway in an uncertain environment). Briefly, it may be said that it is more important to be precisely wrong (though consistently over all subunits) than to be roughly right (with a dispersion of varying subunit estimates of common organization parameters). The coordinative power of budgeting and the corresponding importance of accounting activity in this integrative process are crucially interrelated (Heckert and Willson, 1967: 33-48; Koontz and O'Donnell, 1968: 94-107; and Cyert and March, 1963: 120).[8]

iii. A plan is a theory.--For instance, the budget is built on relationships between factors such as sales and costs on the one hand and profits on the other. This allows the use of sales and cost data as predictors toward the making of an acceptable level of profit. Interestingly, although monthly profit and loss statements or their equivalent (such as contribution margin or like indicators) for subunits are almost universally produced in large firms, their use is less widespread or significant than might be expected. Due to the accounting difficulties and complexities involved in segmented short-run profit statements (particularly in overhead allocation), many operating executives seem to rely more on other plan-oriented performance indicators (Simon *et al*, 1954: 42).

iv. A plan is a precedent.--By the existence of budgets from one year to the next, there is a presumption that existing decisions will be continued. It is exceptional, and due often to extreme duress, for firms to radically re-evaluate the rationale of existing functions. Particularly, this seems most true for "indirect" activities such as advertising, research and development functions, etc.

Due to these features of planning, decisions in the firm tend more than otherwise to have a regularity and consistency over time. Plans, like other standard operating procedures, render a complex set of conditions more simple in appearance. To a major degree, the organization substitutes the plan for the complex and uncertain actual world. To some extent this is done by making the world conform to the plan, partly by acting as if it indeed does providing that levels of performance continue to be satisfactory, budgetary decisions derive predominantly from those of the previous year, without systematic reappraisement from afresh. This reflects the coordinative force of a set of models and assumptions shared by organization members, reinforced by multiple repetition over lengthy stretches of time. The large role and great importance of accounting activities in this process are especially striking.

The discussion above focused mainly on coordination by standardization, particularly through a,counting activities. It is also evident that accounting functions are importantly involved in other techniques of coordination and integration. For instance, in the study of Simon *et al* (1954) of the controller's department, we can find several integrative devices that appear to be prime examples of those in the Lawrence and Lorsch model. To cite a few of these, we commence with the following quotations. "It is essential for the controller's department to develop direct and active channels of communication with the operating executives at those points in the organization where operations are being measured" (Simon *et al*, 1954: 3). " . . . the accounting personnel who are responsible for recording and classifying data need to be as close as possible to the operating situations where the data originate" (Simon *et al*, 1954: 7). These statements seem to be closely reconcilable with the Lawrence and Lorsch concept that more effective integration results from the location of influence at the requisite level, i.e., the position where the necessary knowledge and information for decision-making were available (Lawrence and Lorsch, 1967: 71-73).

Simon *et al* (1954: 6) state that among the most important channels of communication between the controller's and operating departments are "those between the controller and the factory department head, the factory manager, the district and regional sales managers, and the top company executives responsible for production and sales." This implies a strong integrative activity on the part of the controller's department, both "vertically" and "horizontally" in the organization.

Further, it is recommended that divisional controllers (or, equivalently for present purposes, factory controllers or district office managers) should be responsible both to the company controller ("functional" responsibility) and to the factory manager ("administrative" responsibility) in organizations "where top executives of the operating departments regard the controller's services as important management tools" (Simon *et al*, 1954: 8). This system of divided responsibility also implies an integrative function for the divisional controllers. Moreover, the qualifier in the above quote about the top operating executives regarding the controller's services as important management tools appears to fit with the Lawrence and Lorsch finding that integration is more effective when the influence of integrators is higher. This impression is reinforced by the observation that " . . . the greatest service was provided to factory management when the factory accountant felt that he had *authority* to provide reports to the factory management as requested . . ." (Simon *et al*, 1954: 8, emphasis added).

We recall the point of divided responsibility of divisional controllers in connection with the note "Whatever the formal arrangements, it seemed that appointments and removals of factory accountants are almost always a matter of negotiation and agreement between the controller's department and the factory manager" (Simon *et al*, 1954: 9). This seems consistent with the Lawrence and Lorsch finding that the effectiveness of an integrator would tend to be increased if he were to perceive his rewards to flow from both departments (the company controller's and the factory manager's) rather than from one alone. However, we must temper this by a recommendation--not a strong one, though--that factory accountants should tend to look to the controller's department for promotions and salary increases (Simon *et al*, 1954: 84-85). This is somewhat at variance with the Lawrence and Lorsch reward concept. On the other hand, the recommendation is not strongly asserted, and its merit is questioned in later pages (Simon *et al*, 1954: 93-96).

Another suggestion is related to the development of accounting personnel. Recommended are policies for the horizontal transfer of accounting personnel at several stages in their careers (between analytic positions and supervisory positions in record-keeping units), for training prior to and during employment to deepen and broaden their comprehension of general business problems, and for furthering the opportunities for interdepartmental promotions (Simon *et al*, 1954: 9). These suggestions all seem to advance the Lawrence and Lorsch recommendation that integrators are most effective when their personal orientations are intermediate between the departments concerned, rather than extreme. The policies suggested all seem aimed at reducing the narrowness of specialized viewpoint of accountants, and influencing their orientations to more intermediate levels relative to other organizational subunits.

Finally, it is suggested " . . . to encourage the use of teams and 'task forces' drawn from several departments . . ." (Simon *et al*, 1954: 9), which seems to agree with Lawrence and Lorsch when the latter recognize the integrative device of "cross-functional teams".

It can be added that Athreya (1970) studied the long range planning activity as an integrative function, and found it can serve in this capacity. He also made findings with respect to the personal orientations of planners relative to their integrative effectiveness. To the extent that accountants take part in this activity, as Simon *et al* (1954: 9) recommend, Athreya's work has direct bearing on our present discussion. Generally, his results are totally consistent with and supportive of the Lawrence and Lorsch criteria for effective integrative devices and processes.

We conclude that accounting processes are vitally involved in the integrative activity, not only through standardization, but also through the operation of other coordinative and integrative devices as described by Lawrence and Lorsch and by Thompson. It is clear that this has been well recognized in the literature or organization theory, although little dealt with in the accounting literature. The need for synthesis is therefore apparent and seems to offer a useful and important area for accounting research.

GOAL CONGRUENCE

"Goal congruence" is a concept given heavy emphasis in the accounting literature. The term is usually applied to a managerial accounting and control system, emphasizing that it should, so far as possible, influence subunits when acting in their own best interests also to be doing what is most beneficial for the organization as a whole. This premise is that there should be as much congruence as can be achieved between the goals of individual subunits and those of the total organization. See, for example, Anthony, Dearden, and Vancil (196 : 646), Caplan (1971: 58-64), Anthony (1965: 88, 113) and Horngren (1967: 282-283) who states that "the aim is to get subgoals into congruence . . . The greatest danger is overemphasis on one goal which leads to failure to attain other goals". Horngren also recognizes that "overemphasis on multi-goals may lead to diffusion of effort and frustration of efficiency". He suggests that goal congruence is enhanced by the use of techniques for coordination.

While recognizing the general nature of the "goal congruence" problem, the accounting literature is not specific with relation to the particular factors involved, the nature of the processes involved, and the relative effectiveness of various coordination devices under different conditions. By turning to the literature of organization theory it is possible to find some more specific treatments of the subject.

A starting point is to face the problem that individual persons have goals but--without some such postulate as an "organizational mind"--

groups of persons cannot *a priori* be assumed to have goals. One approach is to regard an organization as subservient to one omnipotent person whose goals automatically become those of the organization. Conformity is purchased by payments made to the staff and clear orders handed down for their activities. This approach is characteristic of some theories of management, of the classical economic theory of the firm, and of some accounting authors.

An alternative also found is the assumption of a shared or consensual goal. In the view of Cyert and March (1963: 28)

> Neither solution is entirely happy. Both attempt to define a joint preference ordering for the coalition. In our view, such attempts are misdirected. Actual organizational goals cannot normally be described in terms of a joint preference ordering. Studies of organizational objectives suggest that agreement on objectives is usually agreement on highly ambiguous goals. Such agreement is undoubtedly important to choice within the organization, but it is far from the clear preference ordering usually assumed. The studies suggest further that behind this agreement on rather vague objectives there is considerable disagreement and uncertainty about subgoals, that organizations appear to be pursuing different goals at the same time. (Footnote citations in original omitted.)

Cyert and March conclude that, for business firms, goals are "a series of more or less independent constraints imposed on the organization through a process of bargaining between potential coalition members and elaborated over time in response to short-run pressures. Goals arise in such a form because the firm is, in fact, a coalition of participants with disparate demands, changing foci of attention, and limited ability to attend to all organization problems simultaneously" (Cyert and March, 1963: 43).

Organizational conflict is not fully resolved by these factors. However, despite the existence of goal conflicts, decision-making usually is able to take place due to its decentralization (together with goal differentiation), sequential attention to goals (which helps avoid their inconsistency), and adjustments in organizational slack.[9] The process of organizational goal formation through bargaining is continuously in operation. However, it is rendered more stable than otherwise through various factors. Coalition members are motivated to preserve agreements, notwithstanding unforeseen contingencies, and mutual control systems emerge to protect and enforce past commitments. As Cyert and March (1963: 33) point out

> One such mutual control-system in many organizations is the budget. A budget is an explicit elaboration of previous commitments. Although it is usually viewed as an asymmetric control-device (i.e., a means for superiors to control subordinates) it is clear that it represents a form of mutual control--just as there are usually costs to the department in exceeding the budget, so also are there severe costs to other members of the coalition if the budget is not paid in full. As a result, budgets in every organization tend to be self-confirming.

We recognize that Cyert and March have avoided the danger of "personifying the organization by attributing to its goals. Also, they escape the other extreme of asserting that the goals of an organization are simply those, in some concerted arrangement, of its members. They conclude that "side payments, far from being the incidental distribution of a fixed, transferable booty, represent the central process of goal specification. That is, a significant number of these payments are in the form of policy commitments" (Cyert and March, 1963: 30).

This view is built on further. Thompson (1967) introduces the concept of a *dominant coalition*, or inner circle (pp. 34-36) and of a *domain* (p. 26), which is the set of claims which an organization stakes out for itself in terms of the nature of its product (the goods and/or services it puts out) and the population it serves. Thompson (1967: 26) points out that similar-seeming organizations may differ considerably with respect to domain: " . . . universities are universities, but their domains may range considerably; some offer astronomy courses, others do not; some serve local populations, others are international . . . No two firms in the oil industry are identical in terms of domain. Some refine petroleum, and market gasoline . . . others buy and market gasoline and oil . . ."

Thompson (1967: 128) uses these concepts to consider goals of the organization as

> the *future domains intended by those in the dominant coalition.* Almost inevitably this includes organizational members, but it also may include significant outsiders . . . The view of organization goals presented here overcomes both of the traditional problems; we have not reified the organization, nor have we simply added the preferences of all members. In this view, organization goals are established by individuals--but interdependent individuals who collectively have sufficient control of organizational resources to commit them in certain directions, and to withhold them from others . . . This view also gives us a way of plausibly explaining the often-noted tendency of organizations to seek survival and growth. So long as the organization presents favorable spheres of action to individuals in highly discretionary jobs, we have a strong motivation for them to avoid decisions which would end those spheres of action. If we make the additional assumptions that generations will usually overlap in the dominant coalition, we have the necessary bases for expecting perpetuation of the organization beyond the effective life span of an individual.

Thus, we see that we can reasonably speak of "organizational goals", provided that we understand both the temporary character of the term and the process of goal formation, and do not "reify the organization", as it is easy to slip into doing. It follows that the concept of "goal congruence" is more operationally viewed by considering it in the Lawrence and Lorsch framework of differentiation and integration. In particular, the integrative devices, structures, and processes can, it seems, serve as a desired but not previously-used theoretical underpinning for the accounting "goal congruence" notion. Processes of conflict resolution, cross-functional teams, location of influence at the requisite level, and so on can thus be understood as attempts to enhance goal congruence. More to the point, perhaps, goal congruence emerges as a theoretically viable concept understood in the light of these processes. Not only does introduction of the integrative framework allow understanding and theoretical development of the simplistic notion of "goal congruence", but to this writer it strikingly exemplifies the need for and profit ensuing from joining the literatures of accounting and organization theory.

Another aspect of this issue of organizational and personal goals is discussed by Filley and House (1969: 132), "Any manager, asked if he agrees that a clear statement of organizational and personal objectives is basic to successful organizational performance, would doubtless answer 'yes'. Yet there is a good deal of evidence to suggest that this obvious proposition is not so easy to practice as it is to proclaim."

Research by Maier *et al* (1961) found that there was widespread failure of managers at high levels to share with their subordinates clear understanding of organizational objectives. This problem of poor communication suggests that successive layers in the hierarchy would tend to operate inefficiently and disparately. It may be characterized as a failure to make objectives *operational*, specifying clear goals for subunits and members of the organization.

This incomplete understanding of the need to render objectives operational may be seen in the tendency among administrators to confuse objectives with the standard operating procedures used in the attainment of objectives. This lack of distinction between, or reversal of, ends and means, is not uncommon in bureaucratic-type organization. It may even be the characteristic feature of "bureaucratization".

Filley and House (1969: 137-143) recommend "management by objectives" as one means of establishing operational objectives. This involves the joint participation of superiors and subordinates in defining common objectives, spelling out each individual's major responsibilities in terms of expected performance attainments, and use of these measures as operating guides and in the assessment of performance.

Two propositions are advanced, which tend to be supported by the research evidence: "A clear statement of the organizational objectives to which an individual is expected to contribute directly improves individual performance and coordinated group action by directing individual contributions and encouraging cooperative effort." (Filley and House, 1969: 148) "When attainment of organizational objectives is a means to attainment of personal objectives by the members of an organization, member motivation to work and member satisfaction with the organization will be high." (Filley and House, 1969: 153)

While not doubting the general value of these propositions, we probably would do well to bear in mind the effect of different conditions as illustrated in the Lawrence and Lorsch model, and to recall that a contingency theory of organizations seems to be strongly supported. Hence, circumstances will tend to alter cases, and "single best methods" under all situations will tend to be rare. For example, personality factors have been shown to have important influence in a management-by-objectives program (Carroll and Tosi, 1970).

SUMMARY AND CONCLUSIONS

In reviewing the Lawrence and Lorsch model, it appeared to provide a comprehensive and consistent framework of organization theory. In particular, devices for integration were seen to depend on differentiation, and to be numerous and varied and to be associated with the quality of economic performance. Approached from the standpoint of interdependence rather than differentiation of subunits, the Thompson models of coordination were consistent with and useful extensions of the integration framework.

It was found that coordination was a central and important foucs in the accounting literature. Also, the accounting references to coordination were completely compatible with those of organization theory. While accounting functions were found to play a vital, essential part in the coordination process, the accounting literature on this subject was not sufficiently specific, comprehensive, or rigorous. More operational, detailed, and reliable treatments--heavily involving accounting functions--were shown to be available in the organization theory literature. The accounting processes of coordination were therein seen to reflect the organization theory models of coordinative techniques and integrative devices. Important areas for further accounting research on this subject were noted.

The highly-emphasized accounting concept of "goal congruence" was also examined. It was found to be in need of sharpening and explanation, which was available in the work of Cyert and March and Thompson. This led us back to goal congruence as reflecting an overly simplified concept, which could better be viewed as the complex and comprehensive integrative and conflict-resolution process in the Lawrence and Lorsch framework.

The work of Filley and House were used to examine the problem of poorly-communicated objectives and the bureaucratic phenomenon of "ends-means reversal". It was suggested that "management by objectives" clarification of goals, and the linking of organizational goals with personal objectives of members were likely to promote organizational effectiveness.

NOTES

1. "Boundary-spanning" refers to subunits open to environmental constraints and contingencies instead of being restricted to intra-organizational transactions.
2. In their field study of production, research, and sales departments in six organizations in the plastics industry.
3. Ridgeway (1956) contrasts the disadvantages of single and multiple quantitative criteria for performance measurement and also discusses the use of weighting systems to construct multi-factor composite measures. Each approach is seen as having undesirable consequences and more research into the behavioral consequences of performance measurements is called for.
4. For details of scale construction, see Lawrence and Lorsch (1967), Methodological Appendix, p. 258.
5. Based on increases over the past five years in profits, sales volume, and percent of sales due to new products.
6. Integration was measured by questionnaire responses evaluating the quality of interdepartmental relations on a seven-point scale (Lawrence and Lorsch, 1967: 47, 250-260).
7. For different views see Anthony (1965) and Carter (1971).
8. A vivid description in detail of one company's activities in this area is given in the Empire Glass Cases (A and B) in Dalton and Lawrence (1971: 114-158).
9. The concept of "organizational slack" is described in Cyert and March, 1963: 36-38.

REFERENCES

Anthony, Robert N., "Closing the Loop Between Planning and Performance", *Public Administration Review*, May-June 1971, pp. 388-398.

Anthony, Robert N., John Dearden, and Robert Vancil *Management Control Systems* (Homewood, Ill.: Richard D. Irwin, Inc., 1965).

Anthony, Robert N., *Planning and Control Systems: A Framework for Analysis* (Boston, Mass.: Graduate School of Business Administration, Harvard University, 1965).

Anthony, Robert N., *Management Accounting*, 4th edition (Homewood, Ill.: Richard D. Irwin, Inc., 1970).

Athreya, Mrityunjay, "Planning as Integration", in Lorsch, Jay W. and Paul R. Lawrence *Studies in Organizational Design* (Homewood, Ill.: Irwin-Dorsey, 1970).

Bourque, Donald D., "Information Systems, Reports, and Controls", in Wixon, Rufus, Walter G. Kell, and Norton M. Bedford (editors) *Accountants' Handbook*, fifth edition (New York: The Ronald Press Company, 1970).

Burns, Tom and G. M. Stalker. *The Management of Innovation* (London: Tavistack Publications, 1961).

Caplan, Edwin H., *Management Accounting and Behavioral Science* (Reading, Mass.: Addison-Wesley Publishing Company, 1971).

Carroll, Stephen J., Jr. and Henry L. Tosi, "Gaol Characteristics and Personality Factors in a Management-by-Objectives Program", *Administrative Science Quarterly*, September 1970, pp. 295-305.

Carter, E. Eugene, "The Behavioral Theory of the Firm and Top-Level Corporate Decisions", *Administrative Science Quarterly*, December 1971, pp. 413-428.

Chandler, Alfred D., Jr. *Strategy and Structure* (Cambridge, Mass.: The M. I. T. Press, 1962).

Copeland, Ronald M., "Consolidated Statements", in Wixon, Rufus, Walter G. Kell, and Norton M. Bedford (editors) *Accountants' Handbook*, fifth edition (New York: The Ronald Press Company, 1970).

Cyert, Richard M. and James G. March. *A Behavioral Theory of the Firm* (Englewood Cliffs, N. J.: Prentice-Hall, Inc., 1963).

Dalton, Gene W. and Paul R. Lawrence, editors. *Motivation and Control in Organizations* (Homewood, Ill.: Irwin-Dorsey, 1971).

Dearborn, Dewitt C. and Herbert A. Simon, "Selective Perception: A Note on the Departmental Identifications of Executives", *Sociometry*, June 1958, pp. 140-144.

Dill, William R., "Environment as an Influence on Managerial Autonomy", *Administrative Science Quarterly*, March 1958, pp. 409-443.

Fiedler, Fred E., "Technical Report No. 10", Group Effectiveness Research Laboratory, University of Illinois, 1962.

Filley, Alan C. and Robert J. House. *Managerial Process and Organizational Behavior* (Glenview, Ill.: Scott, Foresman and Company, 1969).

Golembiewski, Robert T., "Comments", Proceedings of *Symposium on Behavioral Experiments in Accounting*, Ohio State University, 1972.

Heckert, J. Brooks and James D. Willson. *Business Budgeting and Control*, 3rd edition (New York: The Ronald Press Company, 1967).

Hickson, David J., D. S. Pugh, and Diana C. Pheysey, "Operations Technology and Organization Structure: An Empirical Reappraisal", *Administrative Science Quarterly*, September 1969, pp. 378-397.

Horngren, Charles T. *Cost Accounting: A Managerial Emphasis*, 2nd edition (Englewood Cliffs, N. J.: Prentice-Hall, Inc., 1967).

Kast, Fremont E. and James E. Rosenzweig. *Organization and Management* (New York: McGraw-Hill Book Company, 1970).

Koontz, Harold and Cyril O'Donnell. *Principles of Management*, 4th edition (New York: McGraw-Hill Book Company, 1968).

Lawler, Edward E., III, "Comments", Proceedings of *Symposium on Behavioral Experiments in Accounting*, Ohio State University, 1972.

Lawrence, Paul R. and Jay Lorsch. *Organization and Environment* (Boston, Mass.: Graduate School of Business Administration, Harvard University, 1967).

Leavitt, Harold J., "Unhuman Organizations", *Harvard Business Review*, July-August 1962, pp. 90-98.

Likert, Rensis. *New Patterns of Management* (New York: McGraw-Hill Book Company, 1961).

Maier, N. R. F., R. L. Hoffman, and W. H. Read. *Superior-Subordinate Communication in Management* (New York: American Management Association, 1961).

March, James G. and Herbert A. Simon. *Organizations* (New York: John Wiley and Sons, Inc., 1958).

Mohr, Lawrence B., "Organizational Technology and Organizational Structure", *Administrative Science Quarterly*, December 1971, pp. 444-459.

Ridgeway, Valentine F., "Dysfunctional Consequences of Performance Measurements", *Administrative Science Quarterly*, September 1956, pp. 240-247.

Simon, Herbert A. *Models of Man* (New York: John Wiley and Sons, Inc., 1957).

Simon, Herbert A., Harold Guetzkow, George Kozmetsky, and Gordon Tyndall. *Centralization versus Decentralization on Organizing the Controller's Department* (New York: Controllership Foundation, now the Financial Executives Institute Research Foundation, Inc., 1954).

Smith, Claggett G. and Oguz N. Ari, "Organizational Structure and Member Consensus", *American Journal of Sociology*, May 1964, pp. 623-638.

Thompson, James D. *Organizations in Action* (New York: McGraw-Hill Book Company, 1967).

Udy, Stanley, "Administrative Rationality, Social Setting and Organizational Development", in Cooper, W. W., H. J. Leavitt, and M. W. Shelley, II (editors). *New Perspectives in Organization Research* (New York: John Wiley and Sons, Inc., 1964).

Welsch, Glenn A. *Budgeting: Profit Planning and Control*, 3rd edition (Englewood Cliffs, N. J.: Prentice-Hall, Inc., 1971).

Wixon, Rufus, Walter G. Kell, and Norton M. Bedford, editorial consultants. *Accountants' Handbook*, 5th edition (New York: The Ronald Press Company, 1970).

Woodward, Joan. *Industrial Organization: Theory and Practice* (Oxford, England: Oxford University Press, 1965).

Accounting for Inflation: Implications for Regulated Industries

Concern with the accelerated rate of inflation pervades all sectors of our economy. Nowhere is this concern more apparent than among regulated public utilities. While unregulated firms, however reluctantly, often are able to pass on higher prices to the consumer, the regulated firm must petition its public utility commission for indemnification against inflation. The process is slow and the ultimate regulatory decision rarely satisfies the generally conflicting interests of both public utility investors and consumers. The normally difficult question of what constitutes a "fair return" becomes considerably more complex when the effects of inflation are introduced into the analysis.

The question of inflation in a regulatory context involves a "primary" and a "secondary" issue. These issues need to be clearly distinguished so that the inevitable confusion which arises from viewing them interchangeably may be avoided. Bonbright states the primary issue as follows:

> The primary issue is that between those persons who contend, and those persons who deny, that the 'fair return' - to public utility companies is a return designed to compensate the corporate stockholder for any deterioration (or any *major* deterioration) in the purchasing power of the dollar that has occurred between the time of the original capital investment and the time of a rate case.[1]

It is not the main purpose here to advance detailed arguments for and against compensating the stockholder for losses in the purchasing power of the dollar. Such social equity arguments necessarily rest on deeply embedded personal value judgments held by different parties of interest and are not easily resolved by an appeal to economic rationality.

A more practicable course is to acknowledge that as the rate of inflation increases there is a corresponding increase in pressure on regulatory commissions to consider past and anticipated losses in stockholder purchasing power in ratemaking decisions. Although their underlying analysis is rarely explicit or apparent, there is reason to believe that public utility commissions do in fact attempt to compensate stockholders in varying degrees for inflation losses by either upward adjustments in the rate base or increases in the allowed rate of return or both. As a consequence, the "secondary" issue of determining relevant information requirements for regulators under inflationary conditions has become a key issue in rate cases. It is this issue that we will be principally concerned with in this paper.

Before directly considering information requirements of public utility commissions, a brief review of regulatory philosophy and procedure will be offered in the first two sections of this paper. Since the ultimate output of rate regulation, the rate of return, is determined by two accounting variables (earnings and rate base assets), the third section of the paper will be devoted to a critical examination of alternative accounting constructs that have been developed to deal with price inflation with special reference to public utility rate regulation. The fourth section of the paper is addressed to the fundamental question of whether the accounting rate of return model currently used in regulatory decision making is in fact the appropriate vehicle for achieving the basic objectives of regulation. In the last section of the paper some alternative constructs are presented and suggestions for research priorities are offered.

REGULATORY DECISION MAKING

Regulators in this country use a remarkably simple framework to administer a public utility environment which is equally remarkable for its pervasiveness and complexity. The far reaching impact of a decision by a public utility commission was recently described by Lerner and Moag:

> When a regulator makes a decision that a particular expenditure constitutes an appropriate increment to a public utility's rate base, his action affects the firm, its shareholders, and the surrounding economy. His decision may enable the firm to combine resources in a more efficient manner, or it may allow inefficiencies to be preserved in the production process. It may lead to windfall gains by shareholders or to the frustration of their legitimate expectations. It may allow a community to expand and thrive, or it may impose so high a cost upon the area that its future growth is limited.[2]

The extent to which each of the foregoing factors are considered in regulatory decision making is not clear. There seems to be little basis for making valid generalizations about the underlying details of regulatory decision models. At present we have the seemingly incongruous combination of abstract, philosophical guidelines serving in a very general way as inputs into a simple, but very specific, rate-of-return construct. We will return to the question of whether an accounting rate-of-return model serves as an effective instrument of regulatory objectives in a later section of the paper. At this point, we propose to review very briefly some of the major criteria used in rate regulation and, in addition, to describe the use of the rate-of-return model as a regulatory vehicle, particularly under conditions of inflation.

When discussing major factors which should determine a fair return, the ability to attract required capital is invariably mentioned by writers in the public utility field. Since capital attraction is crucial for uninterrupted service to the public, there can be little argument with this proposition in principle. The debate arises when consideration is given to specific levels of return actually needed to attract capital. There is additionally the critical question of what is meant operationally by the term "return". The capital attraction criterion is a particularly significant issue in an inflationary setting. As Bonbright points out, "the question [of] whether existing investors have a fair claim to indemnity for *past* inflation may be held to depend on the question [of] whether uncommitted prospective investors are willing to supply new capital without receiving any protection against *future* inflation."[3]

A function of regulation closely related to capital attraction is balancing the interests of the utility's investors and its customers. Ideally rates should be set at a level which efficiently provides customers with required services while allowing the company's earnings to be maintained at a competitive risk-return level with other industries. Once again the guideline is relatively non-controversial while the details of its implementation are not so apparent. Other criteria that should perhaps be considered in rate-setting policy, such as stimulating managerial efficiency and rationing of new services among those for which consumers are willing to pay at least the incremental costs, have been recommended by writers in the field.[4] Here the regulator is involved in extremely complex public policy issues. Indeed, the very act of setting rates that assure a company a fair rate of return without regard to whether it is an efficient producer or a poorly managed company may mitigate against the objective of stimulating managerial efficiency. Recognizing that each of the interdependent criteria discussed here represent important elements in an overall rate-setting policy, we are now prepared to examine the rate-of-return model as an instrument to achieve the aims of regulation in an inflationary setting.

REGULATORY CONCEPTS OF RATE OF RETURN

The rate of return model used by utility commissions in this country is generally defined as the ratio of net operating revenue after taxes but before interest deductions to the rate base. The rate base is composed of depreciated investments in utility plant plus an allowed level of working capital. The rate structure for customers and revenues for the utility thus depend upon the value assigned to the rate base and the rate-of-return allowed on that rate base by the utility commission. That cost of service is a generally accepted and guiding basis for regulatory rate setting is apparent from the indentity:

cost of service or revenue requirements = operating expenses (including depreciation and taxes) + return on rate base

What, of course, is not so clear is what properly constitutes the relevant cost of service. Here we are faced with two basic issues:

1. Is the rate of return on rate base equivalent to the cost of the utility's capital or alternatively the market rate-of-return required to attract sufficient funds to the utility? If not, are there known transformation functions which allow a regulator to determine the return-on-rate base needed to achieve desired levels of returns to the utility investor?
2. Assuming that there is an affirmative answer to one of the two questions posed above, what is the appropriate basis for valuing the rate base?[5]

There appears to be a tacit acceptance in the public utility field that rate base returns can either be equated to or transformed to yield given levels of investor returns. Because of major differences in the models used to calculate the investor's return and the utility rate base return, one should at minimum seriously question the validity of this assumption. We will in fact do exactly that in a subsequent section of the paper. We will propose at that time that differences in the logical forms of the models are necessary but not sufficient grounds for rejecting the equivalence of the two returns, since ultimately the proposition must stand the test of rigorous empirical validation. Since, to my knowledge, no such research is generally available, for purpose of the discussion to follow it will be reluctantly and temporarily assumed that rate base returns can indeed be equated to or transformed to yield given levels of investor returns.

Having accepted for the moment the regulator's implied framework, the question of alternative approaches to valuing the rate base is now pertinent. At present three rate base valuation methods are used by commissions.

1. Original cost: the historical cost of property when first placed into public service, less depreciation.
2. Reproduction cost: the cost, at present prices, of reproducing the existing facilities, less depreciation.
3. Fair value: a value, determined by public utility commissions, which is somewhere in the range between original cost and reproduction cost.

Once one is prepared to accept the proposition that utility rate base returns can be equated to comparable levels of return to stockholders, the grounds for supporting an original cost rate become less difficult to explain. In the absence of inflation and technological advances, it might be argued that the original-cost rate base does in fact represent the approximate value of facilities committed to public service upon which a reasonable rate of return should be earned.[6] Where inflation and technological advances are mutually offsetting or when the rate of inflation is relatively modest, a similar rationale may be proposed in support of an original-cost rate base. In the event that the rate of inflation is substantially greater than partially offsetting technological advances in utility plants, the advocacy of original cost must necessarily rest upon a different line of reasoning. Here the argument for original cost may be either that there is no economic necessity to provide utility investors any protection against inflation for purposes of attracting capital or that as a matter of social equity utility investors merit no relief from inflation since it is not generally available to other investors in the economy.

Reproduction cost is one method used by commissions to adjust for the effects of inflation. The dominant reproduction concept is one which involves estimating the cost of reproducing existing facilities minus depreciation. Since the costs measured in this case are the costs of input factors for facilities, this concept will be hereafter referred to as "input reproduction". A second approach to reproduction is to determine to present cost of producing new facilities to perform the same level of service as existing facilities minus depreciation. Since this approach is oriented toward the output capacity of facilities, it will be referred to as "output reproduction". It is important to point out that both input approaches to reproduction are replacement-cost accounting methods and consequently depart from the principle of establishing the rate base solely on actual costs incurred by the utility. This is the case since replacement cost estimates represent hypothetical costs to the utility, not incurred costs at the time of the rate hearings.

In a period of rising prices, the rate base value resulting from the input reproduction approach will naturally be greater than original cost valuation. In a technologically progressive economy the occasion for identically reproducing an existing physical plant would presumably be a rarity. The more general situation among companies including utilities involves the construction of facilities to provide the same or better quality service at a lower real cost per unit of output. A rate base valued according to the output reproduction approach may be either less than or greater than an original cost rate base depending upon whether the rate of technological change has advanced at a greater or lesser rate than inflation.

If one accepts in principle the legitimacy of replacement or reproduction costs for regulatory purposes, the question still remains as to whether the input reproduction or output reproduction approach would be more appropriate. Since cost of service does appear to have wide acceptance as a fundamental basis for setting rates, logic dictates that the rate base is better valued on the basis of current cost, considering technological advances to replicate service (output reproduction approach) than current cost to replicate an existing plant which is unlikely to be replicated (input reproduction approach). Despite the conceptual superiority of the output reproduction approach over the input reproduction approach, the difficult measurement problems associated with the former approach have apparently persuaded regulators to favor the less speculative input reproduction approach.[7] The use of an input reproduction approach in a technologically advancing industry can result in a substantial "overstatement" of estimated reproduction costs. This "overstatement" can be counteracted by the regulator's subjective reduction in the rate of return allowed on the rate base. For example, if the rate base value calculated on the output reproduction cost basis is $125 million and a return of 5.6% is deemed appropriate, then an equivalent return on an input reproduction cost rate base of $140 million would be 5%. Thus if the regulatory commission treated output reproduction cost as the "norm", but the company's property records were restated to reflect input reproduction costs, a reduction in the rate of return from 5.6% to 5% would be called for.

We began the discussion of reproduction cost with the observation that it is used by regulatory bodies as one means of providing relief from inflation to the utility investor. While it is clear that for a constant rate of return utility rates based on input reproduction costs (and in many cases output reproduction costs as well) will be higher than those based on an original cost rate base, we will show that the extent to which stockholders are granted relief from inflation is neither easily discernible nor generalizable from the regulator's rate of return figures.

After the Hope Natural Gas (1944) case a majority of states moved from fair value rate bases to some form of original cost. Because of subsequent postwar inflation, a number of states returned to fair value rate bases. In 1962, Rose[8] reported that fair value in some form governs rate-setting in seventeen states, original cost in thirty states and the District of Columbia, and reproduction cost is used in Ohio. There was virtually no change in these numbers between 1962 and the end of 1967.[9]

A fair-value rate base may be viewed as a weighted average of original cost and reproduction cost rate bases. When the relative weights attached to each are not disclosed, they can be computed if the value of the original cost and reproduction cost rate bases are known. For example, if original cost (OC), reproduction cost (RC), and fair value (FV) are \$100, \$140 and \$115 million, respectively, then the weight given to reproduction cost (w) is:

$$w = \frac{FV-OC}{RC-OC}$$

$$= \frac{115-100}{140-100}$$

$$= .375$$

What justification can be offered for the use of "w" values of greater than zero but less than one? Livingstone[10] suggests that two major arguments for fair value have been proposed in the literature. The first states that the rate base is heavily financed by fixed-interest bonds and fixed-dividend preferred stock, and only the proportion of the rate base financed by common stockholders need be adjusted for price changes. A second rationale for fair value suggests that it is a convenient compromise vehicle for subjectively dividing gains and losses from price changes between stockholders and consumers. Bonbright, a consistent critic of the fair value standard, characterizes it as "eclectic or compromise standard which takes simultaneous account of conflicting measures on the ground that there is 'something to be said' for each of them".[11] The flexibility of fair value has no doubt contributed to its widespread use. On the other hand, the very flexibility allowed by fair value has also contributed to much confusion, controversy, and lack of understanding about the basis for its application from case to case. As with the case of reproduction cost methods, we propose to show that the extent to which stockholders receive indemnification from inflation is not readily apparent from the regulator's rate of return figures computed on a fair value rate base.

Empirical studies covering 15 Bell operating telephone companies, electric utilities, and natural gas distribution utilities offer some further insight into the regulator decision making behavior. These studies conducted by Eiteman,[12] Livingstone,[13] and Culpepper,[14] respectively, consistently show that commissions adopting relatively higher fair-value and reproduction-cost rate bases partially offset the effect of these higher bases by granting lower rates of return than original-cost jurisdictions. When rates of return granted in fair-value and reproduction-cost jurisdictions are adjusted to reflect the equivalent returns on an original-cost rate base, reproduction jurisdictions show the highest returns and original-cost jurisdiction the lowest. Since the equivalent returns for fair-value and reproduction-cost decisions are greater than those for original-cost, the claim that fair-value and reproduction-cost represent methods to protect the stockholder from inflation may be made. Such a contention could well be an overstatement. A more realistic view is to suggest that a stockholder in a utility governed by fair-value or reproduction-cost rate bases is likely to fare better than his counterpart in an original-cost jurisdiction. Once again, the extent of relief from inflation afforded is not easily derived from the regulator's rate-of-return model.

Perhaps, the results of the empirical studies cited here lend further credence to Bonbright's description of the regulatory decision-making process.

Especially in fair-value jurisdictions, some of the decisions lead one to suspect that the commissions have first reached a conclusion as to reasonable revenue requirements in terms of dollars per annum and then have proceeded to translate these requirements into whatever combination of a rate base and a percentage rate of return will be likely to pass muster with the appellate courts or with public sentiment.[15]

INFLATION AND ACCOUNTING MEASUREMENTS

The accounting literature of the past thirty-five years reflects an active concern by the profession to solve the difficult asset and income measurement problems posed by inflation. This period began with Sweeney's[16] landmark contribution in 1936 and culminated with the Accounting Principles Board's (APB) Statement Number 3[17] issued in June 1969. In Statement Number 3, the APB not only reaffirmed its full support for voluntary supplemental disclosure of the financial impact of changing prices, but in addition, provided specific recommendations on how to prepare and present supplemental financial statements restated for *general* price-level changes. It is, of course, too soon to assess the impact of the statement on corporate financial reporting, particularly in light of the SEC's passive role on this issue to date. Nonetheless, because of the influence exercised by the Board, a reasonable speculation is that Statement Number 3 could become an important factor in extending corporate disclosure if the recent rise in the rate of inflation continues.[18] The introduction of new accounting measurements intended to aid investors in resource allocation decisions will undoubtedly influence the type of financial information used in social equity decisions such as public utility regulation. It is for this reason that the accounting profession's dialogue on measurement under conditions of inflation is of particular interest here.

Accountants have expressed an interest in employing both general price-level changes and specific price-level changes for purposes for measuring income and financial position. Conceptually, a general price-level change reflects a change in the value of the monetary unit during periods of inflation and deflation. Specific price-level changes involve changes in the values of individual assets or relatively homogeneous groups of assets owned by a firm. The distinctions between general and specific price-level changes are important both in theory and in differences in techniques of adjustment.

Although there are no known cases in which financial statement presented in an annual report have been completely adjusted for changes in the general price level, with the recent publication of Statement Number 3 we fully expect a number of companies to begin including such presentations in annual reports. General price-level statements, it is often argued, do not depart from the historical cost principle since in general price-level statements historical costs are simply restated for changes in the general purchasing power of the dollar. Two questions need to be considered at this point. What is meant by general purchasing power? And of what relevance are general price-level adjustments to the corporate stockholder concerned about the impact of inflation on his investment?

A change in general purchasing power may be characterized as either an increase or decrease in the ability to consume goods and services with a fixed quantity of money from one period to the next. Ideally, what is required to measure changes in general purchasing power is an index of prices which includes all goods and services in the economy. No such omnibus index exists at present nor is it likely that such an index will be constructed in the immediate future. Deferring for the moment, the question of whether an omnibus index to measure changes in general purchasing power is even approriate, let us briefly consider the indexes proposed by general price-level adjustment advocates. There are three so-called "general" indexes that have been proposed, namely, the Consumer Price Index, the Wholesale Price Index, and the Gross National Product Implicit Price Deflator. Statement Number 3 recommends the use of the Implicit Price Deflator which is issued quarterly by the U.S. Department of Commerce. Contrary to the common assumption that the choice among these three "general" indexes does not matter, "year-by-year comparison will reveal significant divergencies on occasion between the above-mentioned indexes, even to the point where they move in different directions, as during some periods of the war in Korea."[19]

The Implicit Price Deflator, calculated by deflating approximately one-hundred components of GNP by specific indexes, is no doubt the most comprehensive available measure of over-all price movements. Because the procedure for obtaining the Implicit Price Deflator index involves the use of shifting weights among the GNP components, the value of the dollar in various years is defined in terms of different mixes of goods and services. This shortcoming operates against the claim that "general" price-level adjusted statements would be expressed in dollars of the same purchasing power.[20] Neither the Consumer's Price Index nor the Wholesale Price Index quality as measures of change in *general* purchasing power as defined earlier because each is oriented to measuring price changes in a limited sector of the economy.

Having concluded that at present we have no index well suited to monitor changes in general purchasing power, let us now return to the basic question of whether general price-level adjusted financial statements are indeed relevant to the corporate stockholder. Despite almost fastidious attention paid to the details of calculating general price-level adjustments, there is a dearth of theoretical support for the concept itself. The question of whether we should have financial statements adjusted for general price-levels seems to have been abandoned in favor of questions concerning the specific techniques to be employed.[21] There are few who would claim that any of three indexes which might be used for price-level adjustments are intended to reflect changes in the purchasing power of the firm because of the significant differences in the firm's "market basket". If the concept cannot be supported on these grounds, what other justification can there be for general price-level adjustments? General price-level indexes purport to show changes in the value of a dollar, however, such changes affect only those who use money to purchase goods and services. How is the corporate stockholder affected?

> With a general purchasing power concept, it is assumed that the investor had a free choice to spend his money in the economy any way that he wished at the time of his investment, and that when the capital is recovered through the sale of product or services, the investor will again have the freedom to spend his money any way that he wishes. That is, the operating cycle of the business is assumed to flow from cash to nonmonetary assets and back to cash, and the cash is then available to the investor for general spending. *This is a single-venture concept that is not relevant to large corporate enterprises*[22] (emphasis added.)

The stockholder becomes a potential consumer upon receiving dividend payments from the firm and when he liquidates his investment. Assuming that the stockholder has a record of all money flows related to his investment and that he can either construct or use an existing price index to approximate changes in his purchasing power, he can of course compute a price-level adjusted return on his investment. An important input into his computation is the liquidation value of his investment or the price of the stock at the terminal date. Should the price of the stock be determined by the market on the basis of past or expected general price-level adjusted earnings of the company? Adjusted earnings are likely to mislead rather than enlighten the investor, since general price-level adjustments are neither intended nor are they likely to reflect changes in the purchasing power of the firm. Hence, depending upon the differences in rates of inflation between the company's "market basket" and the goods and service mix used to compute the "general" price index, adjusted assets and earnings may be either over-or understated when the purchasing power of the firm is used as a norm.

To date, earnings and rate bases computed on a general price-level adjusted basis have not found acceptance in public utility regulation. In the past this approach has received the endorsement of such respected authorities as Bonbright[23] and Morton[24]. Nonetheless, the commissions have wisely resisted implementing general price-level adjustments. With the recently accelerated rate of inflation and the issuance of Statement Number 3 by the Accounting Principles Board, one can only hope that public utility commissions will consider carefully the critical shortcomings of general price-level adjustments and resist the temptation to employ administrative expediency by using an index for no better reason than its availability.

Up to now we have discussed changes in the general purchasing power of money. Another school of accounting thought, the current cost school, would argue that price changes in the specific assets held by the firm require adjustments in financial statements. A third group purposes that adjustments for both changes in general purchasing power and specific prices are required.[25]

The current cost approach generally involves valuing the firm's assets at either their estimated replacement costs or their "current cash equivalent", that is, the price that might be reasonably obtained if the assets were sold. Chambers,[26] for example, favors the use of the "current cash equivalent" valuation basis, while Edwards and Bell,[27] who are largely responsible for the renewed current-cost interest in the accounting literature, favor replacement cost as the measure of current cost. Many writers in the area seem to support the replacement cost variant of current costing on the grounds "current cash equivalent" is irrelevant for valuing fixed assets since their sale during the normal course of business is not contemplated.[28] For purposes of our analysis here we will consider only the replacement cost basis.

For purposes of establishing a rate base value, the conventional (input) reproduction cost basis used by some regulatory commissions is identical in concept to replacement-cost accounting. Presumably replacement costs are established by either examining current market prices, by appraisal, or by use of price index numbers to adjust the original cost of an asset to a level which approximates the price that would have to be paid currently. The problems associated with valuing a rate base on the replacement costs of assets that are unlikely to be replaced in kind in a technologically advancing industry were presented earlier. Using output reproduction cost as a norm, we know that input reproduction cost will result in an overstatement of the rate base where there has been technological change.

There is one noteworthy difference between replacement-cost accounting and the accounting methods used to determine the earnings numerator in reproduction cost jurisdictions or fair-value jurisdictions where reproduction-cost is part of the fair-value rate base.[29] In replacement-cost accounting depreciation is computed on the basis of the current replacement cost of assets, whereas commissions generally permit depreciation to be computed exclusively on original cost. If replacement-cost accounting were to be completely adopted for regulatory purposes, the "cash earnings" for investment or earnings before depreciation permitted utilities during periods of rising asset prices would be greater than that permitted under the present practice of computing depreciation on an original cost basis. For example, assume that net plant on an original cost basis is $100 and net plant at input reproduction cost is $140. Depreciation for the firm averages 5% of net plant and the public utility commission establishes a 6% return on the reproduction cost rate base. Applying the regulatory and the replacement-cost accounting approaches, respectively, the following results are obtained:

	Net plant - reproduction cost	Depreciation	Permitted earnings	"Cash earnings"
Regulatory approach	$140	$5	$8.4	$13.4
Accountant's approach	140	7	8.4	15.4

Before concluding this section dealing with accounting for inflation, a brief review of the thinking of those who favor adjustments for both changes in general purchasing power and specific prices is warranted. The dominant argument for a dual adjustment is that prices do not move together, and that while general price level adjustments deal with the effects of inflation, specific price adjustments are also necessary to permit the maintenance of real capital. Advocates of dual adjustments almost invariabley point out that neither adjustment is a substitute for the other. In an appendix of Statement Number 3 differences among four different bases of accounting are considered. The four accounting bases are historical cost, historical cost restated for general price-level changes, current cost, and current cost restated for general price-level changes. An example illustrating the results of applying each method is presented as Exhibit A.

An examination of Exhibit A suggests a number of valid generalizations. Restating the income statement for general price-level adjustments changes the amount ($10,000 instead of $14,000) but not the timing of the income reported from that reported under the conventional historical cost basis. Note that on the balance sheet general-price level accounting (column 2) simply applies the general price-level index number against historical cost, while specific price adjustments (column 3) represent replacement cost or current market value of the assets. Specific price adjustments in the income statement change the timing, but not the total amount of income recognized. As one would expect the dual adjustment (column 4) results in changes in both the timing and amount of income recognized.

Exhibit A

Land was purchased in year 1 for $20,000. Market price did not change in year 1.

Land was held during year 2, during which market price advanced to $26,000.

Land was sold for $34,000 at the end of year 3.

GNP Deflator indexes:

Year 1	100
Year 2	110
Year 3	120

	Historical Cost		Current Value	
	Not restated (Col. 1)	Restated (Col. 2)	Not restated (Col. 3)	Restated (Col. 4)
Balance sheet amount of land				
End of year 1	$20,000	$20,000	$20,000	$20,000
End of year 2	$20,000	$22,000	$26,000	$26,000
Year 3 before sale	$20,000	$24,000	$34,000	$34,000
Income statement gains reported				
In year 1	$ –0–	$ –0–	$ –0–	$ –0–
In year 2	–0–	–0–	6,000	4,000(1)
In year 3	14,000	10,000	8,000	5,640(2)
Total gains for 3 years	$14,000	$10,000	$14,000	$10,000(3) (year 3 dollars)

Notes

(1) Market price, end of year 2	$26,000
Restated market from year 1: 20,000 x 110/100 =	22,000
Gain from appreciation	$ 4,000
(2) Selling price, year 3	$34,000
Restated market from year 2: 26,000 x 120/110 =	28,360
Gain from sale	$ 5,640

(3) The $4,000 gain in year 2 must be restated to year 3 dollars.

Total gain:		
Year 2 appreciation–		
In year 2 dollars	$4,000	
In year 3 dollars	$4,000 x 120/110	$ 4,360
Year 3 sale		5,640
Total in year 3 dollars		$10,000

We have previously contended that general price-level accounting is not relevant to the firm since it does not measure changes in the purchasing power of the firm. The stockholder, on the other hand, may find "general" price indexes useful for purposes of adjusting his money flows (investment, dividends, and disinvestment) for changes in his purchasing power. It is, however, essential to point out that the stockholder's price-level adjustment should not be applied to the financial statements of the firm. The problems associated with specific price-level adjustments based on the input reproduction cost principle have also been enumerated earlier. We must, therefore, reluctantly conclude that the dual adjustment approach which combines the limitations of both general and specific price adjustments holds no more promise for the utility regulator than the application of the individual methods separately.

RECONSIDERATION OF THE REGULATORY CONCEPT OF RETURN

Having concluded that both the regulator's fair value - input reproduction cost approach and the accounting profession's general price-level recommendations are lacking as mechanisms for dealing with inflation, we now propose to examine more closely the usefulness of the accounting or book return measure employed by regulatory commissions to achieve their aims. Apart from the question of how to incorporate appropriate recognition of inflation, the accounting rate of return measure has been subjected to two major criticisms when it is used for ratemaking purposes: The first criticism is that the accounting or book rate of return (b) is generally treated as if it were an unbiased measure of cost of capital (k). The second limitation attributed to the regulator's accounting-oriented framework is that it does not fully capture the scope of the regulator's system of interest.

Consider first the latter criticism. Lerner and Moag have argued persuasively that there are at least three serious deficiencies in using the accounting rate-of-return framework as a source of information for regulatory decision making.

> The accounting equations do not explicitly incorporate all of the major variables that are of interest to the regulatory commission. It is obvious, for example, that the level of present and future services does not appear as a formal target variable in the equations used in the decision process. As a consequence of this ommission, there is a real risk that a regulator seeking to administer the price at which services are sold through rate-of-return considerations alone may unknowingly fix other variables of concern, such as outputs or resource uses, at levels which he would deem undesirable.
>
> The variables included in the accounting identities are related to one another in ways other than those implicit in the accounting tautologies. For example, the interest rate (i) is linked to the proportion of debt in the capital structure: as the proportion of debt increases, the rate of interest that the utility must pay for the funds it borrows increases. Operating costs (O) are a function of the level of output (Q) which, in turn, is one component of the total revenue function, and so forth. In general, then, there is a systematic relationship among events in the utility and between the utility and its environment which cannot be captured by the accounting framework.

> There is no decision technology for choosing among alternative states of affairs. Whenever a regulator chooses a certain level of revenues, a certain price, a certain rate of return, or a certain capital structure, that choice will have effects throughout the firm as well as on the environment. Some of the effects will occur in the current period under study; some will occur in future periods. In choosing one variable over another, the regulator is, in effect, choosing one rather complex state of affairs over another. The accounting framework neither allows him to predict the state of affairs which will result from such a decision nor to consider alternative states of affairs before deciding.[30]

In light of these inadequacies, Lerner and Moag suggest a shift from the present rate-of-return framework to one which explicitly recognizes the systems relationships involved for a firm to meet its output requirements. They go on to suggest that this can be viewed as a mathematical programming problem with a cost minimization objective function and constraints that specify output levels and functional relationships that must not be violated.[31] Whether it is economically feasible to develop data inputs of sufficient accuracy to permit the beneficial use of such a programming model most naturally be questioned. The essential validity of the Lerner-Moag criticism of the current framework is however difficult to deny.

Assume that a regulator's response to the foregoing criticism is that while it is true that the rate-of-return framework does not explicitly incorporate all of the systems variables, these variables are in fact considered in deliberations preceding a rate decision. In this case the regulator implies that once the commission establishes future output and mix requirements for the utility, it then employs a combination of setting a rate base and rate which will satisfy the revenue requirements for the desired state of affairs. At this point the regulator is faced with the other major criticism of the conventional framework, i.e. accounting or book rate of return on a utility's rate base is incorrectly treated as if it were an unbiased measure of cost of capital.

Citing a number of Supreme Court rulings, a witness in a rate case for a major public utility argued that the return on rate base to be earned by the utility should be equal to its cost of capital, since any lesser rate would cause the price of the stock to decline.[32] Since k, the cost of capital is generally defined in the finance literature as the minimum return that a firm must earn on an investment to maintain its stock price, it is apparent that the witness has equated b, the book return on a rate base, with k. In fact, the *modus operandi* of regulatory authorities is to estimate k and "translate this number into 'required revenues' by multiplying it against a net book value estimate (or one based on net book value)."[33] Are b and k equivalent? The answer is most assuredly "no". To show that b and k are two distinctly different measures, we will first show that k is a discounted cash-flow (DCF) measure and then summarize some systematic differences between DCF rates-of-return and book rates-of-return.

Although there is no universal definition of cost of capital, a commonly suggested one for public utility rate cases is -

$$k = \frac{D}{P} + g \qquad (1)$$

where D = current dividend

P = current price of the firm's common stock

g = expected rate of growth in dividends

Equation (1) derives from the familiar dividend valuation model -

$$P_o = \frac{D_1}{(1+k)} + \frac{D_2}{(1+k)^2} + \ldots + \frac{D_n}{(1+k)^n} \qquad (2)$$

If dividends are expected to grow at a constant rate, g, then (2) becomes -

$$P_o = \frac{D_1}{(1+k)} + \frac{D_1(1+g)}{(1+k)^2} + \ldots + \frac{D_1(1+g)^{n-1}}{(1+k)^n} \qquad (3)$$

Multiplying both sides of (3) by the expression $\frac{(1+k)}{(1+g)}$ and subtracting (3) from the result we obtain -

$$P_o \frac{(1+k)}{(1+g)} - P = \frac{D_1}{(1+g)} - \frac{D_1(1+g)^{n-1}}{(1+k)^n} \qquad (4)$$

Assuming k > g the right-hand term of (4) approaches zero as n increases. Given a large n, we drop the right-hand term and (4) reduces to -

$$P_o = \frac{D_1}{k-g} \qquad (5)$$

From (5) we obtain the original formulation of k, i.e.

$$k = \frac{D}{P} + g \qquad (1)$$

Thus we conclude that the commonly employed measure of k given by (1) derives from the dividend valuation model (2) in which k is a DCF rate-of-return. Specifically for a known P_o and estimates of the dividend stream, k is the internal rate-of-return or discount rate which equates the future stream of dividends to the present price of the stock.

Having established k as a DCF-derived return, let us review certain essential differences between DCF versus book returns. For purposes of this paper, we distinguish between book return before interest and taxes (b) and the regulatory return (r) computed as follows:

$$r = \frac{\pi=i(L)}{A} (1-T) \qquad (6)$$

where π = net income after interest and taxes

i = average rate of interest paid on outstanding debt

L = outstanding debt

A = net plant T = income tax rate

The suggestion that DCF returns and b are likely to be different for a given investment comes as no surprise in light of the fundamental differences between the models used to compute these two returns. Note that the relevant flows for computing DCF returns are cash flows, while accrual accounting flows are used to obtain values for both the numerator and denominator of b. A second fundamental difference lies in the respective time horizons incorporated in each measure. DCF returns are based on multi-period, prospective flows. Book returns, in contrast, are generally single-period, historical measures.

Soloman[34] has examined the relationship between b and a known internal rate-of-return for a series of identical investment projects as certain basic parameters such as length of project life, timing of cash flows, accounting policies for capitalization and depreciation, investment growth and inflation rates are changed. The essential conclusions of Solomon's study may be summarized as follows:

1. For the basic zero-growth case in which a company's annual investment expenditures are constant over time b overstates the DFC return.
2. As a greater proportion of each project is expensed the divergence between b and DCF return increases. For example, in Solomon's illustration the constant DCF return is 10% and for a policy of 100% capitalization b = 12.6%. For 20% and 50% expensing of investments b = 15.4% and 25.2%, respectively.
3. As a company shifts from straight-line depreciation to accelerated depreciation methods b will increase from the basic case since relatively larger proportions of initial investment are written off early in a project's life. This leads once again to an increased divergence between b and the constant DCF return.
4. The divergence between b and DCF return increases as project life increases. At the limit, when project life is very long b will approach twice the level of the DCF return.
5. The book return, b, is also a function of the time lag between investment outlays and resulting inflows. There may be a lag in the investment project between its inception and completion. Another possibility is a lag between project completion and initial inflow of cash from operations. In general as the lag between investment expenditures and subsequent cash inflows increase, there is a corresponding increase in b over the constant DCF return.
6. Departing from zero-growth assumption, as a company invests at a rising rate, b will be less than the DCF rate for a zero-growth company because the book yield denominator will be more heavily weighted with newer investment projects with relatively higher net book values relative to net income. In the unique case where the rate of growth in investment is identical to the DCF return, b is also equal to the DCF return.
7. Assuming that there is a common rate of inflation for the firm's investment inputs and cash flow outputs, b will overstate the DCF return by a greater margin than in the absence of inflation.

The implications of the foregoing for regulatory commissions are profound. The hazards of employing careful analysis to determine a reasonable k for the utility investor and then treating b as if it were the equivalent of DCF-derived k should by now be apparent. The problem of developing supplementary constructs to deal with inflation further complicates the issue. An understanding that b and k, although both commonly referred to as return on investment, are indeed two different measurements is a prerequisite toward developing improved regulatory frameworks. A modest effort in that direction will be attempted in the following section.

AN ALTERNATIVE APPROACH

We submit at the very outset that a recommended regulatory framework should explicity incorporate systems relationships which link necessary inputs with desired outputs. It is beyond the scope of this paper to consider the details of modeling demand curves, production functions, and all the various functional relationships operating within a firm. Nonetheless, a few words about systems outputs and related input requirements are in order at this point.

Outputs of a public utility may be classified as (1) service outputs to customers, (2) monetary outputs to investors, and (3) social outputs to the community. The difficulty of achieving consistently satisfactory levels for each of these three outputs through time is of course well known to public utilities and regulatory commissions alike. One difficulty stems from the complex problems associated with balancing the conflicting interests among customer, investors, and the community at large. Secondly, the inputs required to establish and maintain acceptable levels of output in all three areas simultaneously may be in short supply. Money and managerial talent come to mind as prime examples of limiting resources for many industrial organizations.

Consider the task of providing service outputs to customers. Customer service has both quantitative and qualitative dimensions. On the quantitative side, the utility must provide enough service outputs to satisfy demand. As the public demands not only basic service, but more comprehensive service, utilities are expected to respond in kind. For example, as the telephone network grows customers may require more and larger directories, better information and intercept service, and more detailed billing arrangements. To meet service output goals the utility must plan three types of capital expenditure inputs: (1) capital expenditures for replacement of existing service; (2) capital expenditures for expansion of capacity; (3) capital expenditures for improvements in service quality. To sustain satisfactory service on a day-to-day basis an appropriate mix of labor, material, and capital inputs must naturally be maintained as well. These inputs may be characterized as the firm's operating expenses.

The second basic public utility output enumerated earlier is monetary outputs to investors. This output is inextricably linked to the customer service output since satisfactory and uninterrupted service depends upon the utility's ability to attract the investor's funds, which in turn depends upon the investor's expectations of future monetary receipts from investing in the firm's shares. Estimating the cost of capital (k) which depends upon stockholder expectations is, as every regulator would undoubtedly attest, a hazardous activity subject to a considerable margin of error. Nonetheless it is a critical step in the rate-making process. When k is defined as $\frac{D}{P} + g$, we see that g, the growth rate of dividends, is the instrumental variable which determines k.[35] Hence, some minimum level of dividends through time must be paid if the utility is to continue to attract capital.

The extent of a utility's responsibility for the social costs of production is a subject of increasing concern to the public. Unquestionably, utilities will spend increasing amounts in the years ahead on research and development and construction aimed at substantially reducing the environmental contamination caused by utility operations. It is too soon to assess the impact of these accelerating costs on utilities, their customers, and investors. It can be confidently stated however, that this "social cost inflation" will rival price inflation as a concern of regulators and certain utilities, particularly electric utilities.

After all of the inputs required to produce acceptable levels of service, monetary, and social outputs have been considered, the potential sources for financing must be taken into account as well. These considerations are summarized in the "Statement of Cash Sources and Requirements" presented as Exhibit B. It should be emphasized that this is a *pro forma* statement and consequently any expected price increases are reflected directly in the cost estimates for each input.

APPENDIX B

Statement of Cash Sources and Requirements

Sources:
- Operating revenues
- Increase in long-term debt
- Proceeds from sale of shares to common stockholders

Requirements:

For service outputs -
- Operating expenses excluding depreciation
- Interest expense
- Tax expense
- Replacement of existing service facilities
- Expansion of capacity
- Improvements in service

For monetary outputs -
- Dividends

For social outputs -
- Research and development
- Construction of environmental control facilities

Once the systems requirements have been estimated, there exists two basic avenues open to the regulator. He may in his analysis wish to retain the conventional rate of return framework, or else he may choose to abandon the conventional framework. We propose to offer a number of simple examples to illustrate how these two basic alternative approaches might be implemented. Adjustments for inflation will be considered as part of the analysis.

Assume that the regulator wishes to continue performing his analysis in the familiar book rate of return framework. Further assume for purposes of this initial example that we are concerned solely with providing a reasonable return to the common stockholder, and that service output to customers and social outputs to the community will be satisfactory levels.[36] The potential dangers in treating book rates of return as if they were equivalent to k, a market-derived *ex ante* measure of stockholders return, have been enumerated earlier. Since g, the growth rate of dividends, is the instrumental variable which determines k, when the regulator sets a level for g, a level of k is implied. Once the g required to produce a desirable level of k is determined, the regulator's rate of return (r) which corresponds to the chosen level of g can be established. Assuming a constant payout ratio, the growth rate of dividends will naturally be identical to the growth rate of earnings. Hence we define g as -

$$g = \frac{\pi_t - \pi_{t-1}}{\pi_{t-1}} \tag{7}$$

where π = net income after interest and taxes

$$\pi_{t-1} = \left(bA_{t-1} - iL_{t-1}\right)\left(1 - T\right) \tag{8}$$

$$\pi_t = \left[bA_{t-1} + b'v\pi_{t-1} + b'v\pi_{t-1}\left(\frac{L_{t-1}}{E_{t-1}}\right) - iL_{t-1} - iv\pi_{t-1}\left(\frac{L_{t-1}}{E_{t-1}}\right)\right] 1 - T \tag{8'}$$

From (7), (8) and (8') we obtain -

$$g = \left(b'v + v\ (b'-i)\ \frac{L_{t-1}}{E_{t-1}}\right)\left(1 - T\right) \tag{7'}$$

where b = book rate of return on assets before interest and taxes
b' = book rate of return on new investment before interest and taxes
A = net plant
i = average rate of interest on outstanding debt
L = outstanding debt
T = income tax rate
v = per cent of net income after interest and taxes reinvested
E = stockholder's equity

Note two assumptions underlying the formulation of equation (8'). First, the constant debt to equity ratio assumption implies that new investment will be financed by retained earnings and new debt in the same proportion as the initial debt to equity ratio in t-1. Secondly, there is the inherent assumption that the level of investment required to maintain current earnings is equal to current depreciation charges.

From equation (7') we obtain a required b' for a given g. To move from b' to the regulator's return, r, we show that -

$$r = \frac{\pi + i\ (L)\ (1-T)}{A} \tag{6}$$

$$= \frac{bA\ (1-T)}{A}$$

$$= b - bT$$

Recognizing the limiting assumptions of the model we now can determine from a g deemed reasonable by the regulator the level of r needed to achieve the chosen g. To illustrate this concept, consider a utility with the following balance sheet at the beginning of year t-1.

Assets	\$1,000,000,000	8% debt	\$400,000,000
		Equity	600,000,000

The company earned \$100,000,000 in t-1. From equations (8) and (6) we know that b = 23.2% and r = 11.6%, respectively. The company has 100,000,000 shares outstanding and a paypout ratio of .4. The market price per share (P) is \$10, thus the company's book and market values are identical. It is estimated that growth expectations for the firm approximate 6%. The cost of capital is 10%, i.e. -

$$k = \frac{(1 - v)}{P/\pi/_S} + g \qquad (1')$$

$$.10 = \frac{(1 - .6)}{10/_1} + .06$$

Assuming a 6% growth rate is judged by the regulator as an appropriate target, what book rate-of-return on new investment (b') must be earned by the firm? From equation (7') we compute -

$$.06 = [(b')(.6) + .6\ (b' - .08)\ 2/3]\ .5$$

$$b' = 15.2\%$$

From equation (6) we obtain the regulator's return on new investment -

$$r' = (.152) - (.152)(.5) = 7.6\%$$

The firm's *pro forma* results for periods t, t + 1, and t + 2 are presented as Appendix C.

APPENDIX C

Pro Forma Income Results (in millions)

	t	t+1	t+2
Last period's net income	\$100.00	\$106.00	\$112.36
Dividends (payout ratio .4)	(40.00)	(42.40)	(44.94)
Reinvested earnings	60.00	63.60	67.42
New debt	40.00	42.40	44.94
Total new capital	\$100.00	\$106.00	\$112.36
Return on new investment (b')	15.2%	15.2%	15.2%
Earnings increase before interest and taxes	15.20	16.11	17.08
Income taxes (50%)	(7.60)	(8.05)	(8.54)
Earnings increase after taxes but before interest	7.60	8.06	8.54
Interest expense - net of taxes	(1.60)	(1.70)	(1.80)
Increase in net income	6.00	6.36	6.74
Last period's net income	100.00	106.00	112.36
Current period net income (g = 6%)	\$106.00	\$112.36	\$119.10

Regulatory commissions have been primarily concerned with average rather than marginal returns. The average return required in any given period is simply the weighted average of the base-period return plus the returns on new investments for each period up to the period of interest. Specifically, the relevant regulator's return is defined as -

$$\hat{r} = \frac{r_{t-1}A_{t-1} + \sum_{t}^{t+n} r'A'}{A_{t-1} + \sum_{t}^{t+n} A'}$$

$$\hat{r}_t = \frac{(.116)(1000) + (.076)(100)}{1000 + 100} = 11.2\%$$

$$\hat{r}_{t+1} = \frac{(.116)(1000) + (.076)(100) + (.076)\ (106)}{1000 + 100 + 106} = 10.9\%$$

$$\hat{r}_{t+2} = \frac{(.116)\ (1000) + (.076)(100) + (.076)(106) + (.076)(112.36)}{1000 + 100 + 106 + 112.36} = 10.6\%$$

Hence, we conclude that an average return on rate base of 11.2%, 10.9% and 10.6% in periods t, t+1, and t+2, respectively would yield a growth rate of 6% which in this hypothetical case was postulated as the rate necessary to attract capital to the utility. Note that $\hat{r}$ declines through time because the marginal return, r', is constant and less than the average yield in period t-1. The regulator who must choose a single average return figure would presumably compute an average $\hat{r}$.

Using the foregoing construct, let us now introduce inflation as an additional variable. Recall that earlier we argued that the current cost to replicate existing plant (input reproduction approach) is not particularly germane to the problem of increasing prices for construction of utility plants. Instead, it was contended that current cost to replicate service outputs (output reproduction cost) giving full recognition to technological advances is relevant to regulatory analysis.

Let χ_t be the ratio of output reproduction cost less original cost to original cost of facilities to be replaced in period t. In the no-inflation example presented earlier in this section it was assumed that the level of investment required to maintain current earnings is equal to the current period's depreciation charges. Employing the output reproduction cost approach, we know that χ% of the current depreciation charge represents the proportion of reinvestment on which no return is earned. This is so since that part of the reinvestment funds must be used to purchase service output capability at higher prices than original cost. With this adjustment for inflation, equation (7') can be reformulated as follows:

$$g = \left[[b'v + v\ (b'-i)\frac{L_{t-1}}{E_{t-1}} - \frac{(\chi_{t-1})\ (N_{t-1})\ (b')]}{\pi_{t-1}} \right] (1-T) \qquad (7'')$$

Suppose depreciation expense, N_{t-1}, is \$50 million and χ = .25. Using equation (7''') we find that b' = 17.4% and therefore r' = 8.7%. The required $\hat{r}$'s for each of the three periods are 11.3%, 11.1%, and 10.9%, respectively. As expected both r' and the $\hat{r}$'s increased from the original-cost case since the same earnings had to be achieved on a lesser amount of productive assets. Specifically, in this case the "no-return" capital assets amount to \$12.5 million or 25% of the \$50 million depreciation expense.[37]

Thus far original cost and reproduction cost illustrations have been presented. Suppose that this case is under consideration in a fari-value jurisdiction and only the proportion of the rate base financed by common stockholders is adjusted for price changes. Equation (7) can now be restated as -

$$g = \left[b'v + v(b'-i)\frac{L_{t-1}}{E_{t-1}} - \frac{(X_{t-1})(N_{t-1})(b')}{\pi_{t-1}} \frac{E_{t-1}}{L_{t-1}+E_{t-1}} \right](1-T) \qquad (7''')$$

As one would expect the r' and $\hat{r}$ values under the fair-value case fall between the corresponding r' and $\hat{r}$ values for original cost and reproduction cost. Using equation (7''') we obtain: r' = 8.2%, $\hat{r}_t$ = 11.29%, $\hat{r}_{t+1}$= 11.0%, and r_{t+2}= 10.8%. The r' and r results for all three cases are summarized in Appendix D.[38]

APPENDIX D

r' and $\hat{r}$'s Required for Three Illustrative Cases

	r'	$\hat{r}_t$	$\hat{r}_{t+1}$	$\hat{r}_{t+2}$
Case 1 - no adjustment for price increases (original cost)	7.6%	11.2%	10.9%	10.6%
Case 2 - with output reproduction cost adjustment	8.7%	11.3%	11.1%	10.9%
Case 3 - with output reproduction cost adjustment for common equity only (fair value)	8.2%	11.29%	11.0%	10.8%

Having illustrated an approach to linking a designated level of k to a required rate of return on the rate base, we are now prepared to illustrate a means of satisfying systems requirements in situations where adherence to the conventional rate of return framework is not considered mandatory. The inputs necessary to produce satisfactory levels of service, monetary, and social outputs are summarized in Appendix B - "Statement of Cash Source and Requirements". Using the variables presented in Appendix B, the regulator's model may be viewed as a revenue minimization formulation subject to the condition that acceptable levels of output are achieved by the utility.

Minimize

$$R_t = D_t + 0_t + C + C' + C'' + I_t + X_t - L' - S'P_t$$

With respect to D, L', S'

Subject to

$L_t \leq .67\ E_t$	Debt/equity constraint
$L_t = L_{t-1} + L'$	Debt linkage
$E_t = E_{t-1} + \pi_t - D_t + S'P_t$	Equity linkage
$\pi_t = (R_t - O_t - N_t - I_t)(1-T)$	Profit
$D_t \geq (D_{t-1}/S_{t-1})\ S_t$	Dividend constraint
$S_t = S_{t-1} + S'$	Common shares linkage
$\pi_t \geq (\pi_{t-1}\ /S_{t-1})\ S_t$	Profit constraint
$N_t = N_{t-1} + .05\ (C+C'+C''-H)$	Depreciation linkage
$I_t = i\ (L_{t-1})+(i'L')$	Interest
$X_t = (R_t - O_t - N_t - I_t)\ T$	Taxes
$P_t = \dfrac{D_{t-1}}{k-g}$	Share price

where

R = revenues

O = operating expenses excluding depreciation

C = capital expenditures for capacity expansion and improvement of service

C'= capital expenditures for social outputs

C'' = capital expenditures for replacement of existing service output

I = interest expense

X = tax expense

L'= new debt, net of retirements

S'= new common shares issued

P = market price of common share

E = stockholders' equity

N = depreciation expense

H = original cost of plant retired

Observe that the following are given or estimated constants: O_t, C, C', C'', D_{t-1}, P_t, H, N_{t-1}, N_t, (π_{t-1}/S_{t-1}), S_{t-1}, (D_{t-1}/S_{t-1}), T, E_{t-1}, and L_{t-1}. Hence, the instrumental variables are D, L', and S'.

The advantages of using an approach which attempts to systematically and explicitly take into account input requirements necessary to achieve satisfaction for customers, investors, and the community can be significant. Regulatory issues become direct rather than indirect. The arguments would no longer hinge on whether a rate base has been properly valued or whether a specified return on a rate base is reasonable. Instead, under the suggested formulation, debate will focus on appropriate levels for the three basic outputs of a utility and parameter estimates of dollar requirements to achieve these outputs. For example, consider the question of inflation. Inflation directly affects expected dollar requirements for operating expenses and capital expenditures, and these expectations should be directly incorporated as parameter estimates in the revenue minimization formulation. The resulting solution then reflects the minimum revenue to obtain certain projected outputs while explicitly recognizing increasing prices for inputs.

The proposed model is naturally more suggestive of a regulatory approach or philosophy than immediately operational. A brief discussion of certain limitations of the model will perhaps be helpful in guiding subsequent research attempts to make it more operational.

First there is the question of the appropriate level of detail. The model presented here is highly aggregated and undoubtedly would obscure important relationships governing the firm. More detailed cost and demand functions for services offered would be particularly helpful when the issue involves not only total revenues required by the utility, but detailed rate structure considerations are involved as well.

The static, single-period model must be extended to a multi-period framework which incorporates dynamic feedback responses between the utility and its environment. For example, how is a given rate change likely to affect demand over the time period under consideration and how will changes in demand affect costs? The introduction of a multi-period framework leads to the question of available means for dealing with uncertainty in key variables affecting utility performance. Much research needs to be done to assess the relevance of statistical decision theory and other management science techniques in the regulatory environment.

Finally, future designs of regulatory models must deal with two extremely difficult problems. First, there is the lag between environmental shifts and regulatory decisions. This suggests that relevant variables in a regulatory analysis are those dealing with the future. The use of historical figures can be helpful only insofar as it aids our understanding of the future. The second problem concerns the conflict between the desirability of establishing reasonably stable rates while at the same time recognizing the need to satisfy the variable requirements of the utility. For example, suppose a utility expects a certain amount of variability in capital requirements during the next few years, to what extent will annual revenue solutions from the proposed model be translatable into a rate structure which meets minimum stability standards? These as well as other important design issues will hopefully receive increasing attention by regulators, utility executives, and educators. Surely, regulatory decisions which have such a profound effect upon the firm, the investment community, and the population at large warrant well-conceived and rigorous research, for the potential benefits from improved analysis can be impressive.

NOTES

1. James C. Bonbright, *Principles of Public Utility Rates*, New York: Columbia University Press, 1961, p. 172.
2. Eugene M. Lerner and Joseph S. Moag, "Information Requirements for Regulatory Decision," in *Rate of Return Under Regulation: New Directions and Perspectives,* edited by Harry M. Trebing and R. Hayden Howard, East Lansing, Michigan: Division of Research, Graduate School of Business Administration, 1969, p. 195.
3. Bonbright, *op. cit.*, p. 267.
4. *Ibid.*, pp. 153-155.
5. There are in addition important issues relating to income determination, such as choice among alternative depreciation methods and accounting for deferred income taxes. These issues have received much attention in both the accounting and public utility literature and will not be considered here.
6. Nonetheless, two questions must necessarily be raised. First, there is the question of whether the application of conventional depreciation methods results in an undepreciated plant balance, which closely approximates the value of the plant at various points in time. Secondly, if the net book value of plant is a good approximation of current value, there is still the more fundamental question of whether return on rate base is an appropriate measure of the stockholder's return.
7. Livingstone suggests a number of measurement issues. First, there is the question of level of aggregation to be used. For example, should it be a single steam turbine, all generating plants for the company, or that of the entire utility plant? In addition, there is the problem of finding a suitable unit of plant output capacity. See John Leslie Livingstone, *The Effects of Alternative Accounting Methods on Regulatory Rate of Return Decision in the Electric Utility Industry*, unpublished doctoral dissertation, Stanford University, 1966, pp. 52-53.
8. Joseph R. Rose, "Confusion in Valuation for Public Utility Rate-Making," *Minnesota Law Review*, Vol. 47, 1962, pp. 2-3.
9. See Charles F. Phillips, Jr., *The Economics of Regulation*, Homewood, Ill.: Richard D. Irwin, Inc., 1969, pp, 272-27.
10. Livingstone, *op. cit.*, pp. 61-62.
11. Bonbright, *op. cit.*, p. 170.
12. David K. Eiteman, "Interdependence of Utility Rate-Base Type, Permitted Rate of Return, and Utility Earnings," *Journal of Finance,* Vol. 17, 1962, pp. 38-52. Eiteman's study covers 15 Bell operating telephone companies from January 1944, the date of the Hope case, to December 1959.
13. Livingstone, *op. cit.* This study involves 90 rate case decisions, from 32 regulatory agencies involving 64 electric utility companies. The period covered begins in January 1954 and ends December 1961. Livingstone also studies the effects of alternative accounting methods.
14. Robert C. Culpepper, "A Study of Some Relationships Between Accounting and Decision-making Processes," *The Accounting Review*, April 1970, pp. 322-332. This study covers the 1954-1961 period and involves 88 decisions reported by 32 regulatory jurisdictions. Sixty-six natural gas companies are represented.
15. Bonbright, *op. cit.*, p. 281.
16. Henry W. Sweeney, *Stabilized Accounting*, Harper & Brothers, 1936. Reprinted in 1964 by Holt, Rinehart and Winston, Inc.
17. "Financial Statements Restated for General-Price Level Changes,"

Statement of the Accounting Principles Board Number 3, New York: American Institute of Certified Public Accountants, June 1969. For a Comprehensive review of price-level accounting through 1963, see Stephen A. Zeff, "Episodes in the Progression of Price-Level Accounting in the United States," *The Accountant's Magazine*, Vol. 68, 1964, pp. 285-304.

18. The change in practice resulting from APB opinion Number 3 issued in October 1963 gives some weight to this speculation. In that opinion the board recommended that funds statements be voluntarily presented as supplementary information in financial reports. This recommendation received the endorsement of the major stock exchanges as well. The impact of the recommendation can be estimated from statistics obtained from the AICPA Annual Survey of the annual reports of 600 industrial and commercial corporations, *Accounting Trends and Techniques*. In 1955 only 21% of the survey companies presented funds statements, while in 1964, 1965, 1966, and 1967 comparable percentages were 65%, 76%, 84%, and 87%, respectively.

19. William H. Hannum and W. Wasserman, "General Adjustments and Price Level Measurement," *The Accounting Review*, April 1968, p. 297.

20. *Ibid.*, pp. 300-301.

21. See, for example, *Reporting the Financial Effects of Price-Level Changes*, Accounting Research Study No. 6, New York: American Institute of Certified Public Accountants, Inc., 1963. For one of the few recent articles challenging the theoretical merits of general price-level adjustments, see John A. Tracy, "A Dissent to the General Price-Level Adjustment Proposal," *The Accounting Review*, January 1965, pp. 163-175.

22. Eldon S. Hendriksen, *Accounting Theory*, revised edition, Homewood, Ill.: Richard D. Irwin, Inc., 1970, p. 224. Further complications arise when the stockholder is an institutional investor whose function is to invest and not to consume. Foreign investors who would find little use in domestic price index pose yet another interesting problem for the application of general price-level adjustments.

23. Bonbright, *op. cit.*, pp. 274-275.

24. Walter A. Morton, "Rate of Return and the Value of Money in Public Utilities," *Land Economies*, May 1952, p. 126.

25. For distinctions among these three schools of thought see Stephen A. Zeff, "Replacement Cost: Member of the Family, Welcome Guest, or Intruder?" *The Accounting Review*, October 1962, pp. 611-625 and Graham Peirson, "Three Kinds of Adjustments for Price Changes," *The Accounting Review*, October 1966, pp. 729-736.

26. Raymond J. Chambers, *Accounting Evaluation and Economic Behavior*, Englewood Cliffs, N. J.: Prentice-Hall, Inc., 1966.

27. Edgar O. Edwards and Philip W. Bell, *The Theory and Measurement of Business Income*, Berkeley and Los Angeles: University of California Press, 1961.

28. For example, see George J. Staubus, "Current Cash Equivalent for Assets," *The Accounting Review*, October 1967, pp. 650-661.

29. In addition there is the question of whether unrealized gains or losses from holding fixed assets properly constitutes a part of the firm's net income.

30. Lerner and Moag, *op. cit.*, p. 198.

31. For an illustration of the programming approach see Eugene M. Lerner and Joseph S. Moag, "Toward an Improved Decision Framework for Public Utility Regulation," *Land Economics*, August 1968, pp. 403-409.

32. Eugene M. Lerner, *Financial Management*, Part I, mimeo, Chapter 12, p. 8.

33. Ezra Solomon, "Alternative Rate of Return Concepts and Their Implications for Utility Regulation," *The Bell Journal of Economics and Management Science*, Spring 1970, p. 79.

34. *Ibid.*, For an earlier, more analytical exposition see "Return on Investment: The Relation of Book Yield to True Yield," in *Research in Accounting Measurement*, eds. Jaidicke, Ijiri, and Nielson, Evanston: American Accounting Association, 1966, pp. 232-244. The basic model assumes constant cash flows, no time lag between investment and the flow of receipts, complete capitalization on all investment outlays, straight-line depreciation, zero salvage value at the end of each project's life, no inflation and beginning-of-year net book values for the denominator of the book rate of return. Depreciation expense is recorded as if all investments are made at mid-year, thus in a "steady state" the undepreciated assets or net book value are simply n(I)/2; where n = project life and I = the investment expenditure. Solomon also uses a before-tax illustration so that cash-flows are unaffected by changes in accounting policies for capitalization and depreciation. While an after-tax basis would change the magnitude of differences between the two measures, the essential relationships would not be affected.

35. The discount rate used by investors, and therefore the present price of the stock, is also a function of important exogenous variables such as interest rates, monetary and fiscal policy, and other factors likely to affect the economy.

36. This latter assumption will be relaxed in the second formulation of the problem presented subsequently.

37. To keep the example simple only price increases in plant costs were considered. A more detailed analysis could, of course, easily incorporate inflation adjustments for the utility's labor and material costs as well.

38. Suppose that an annual inflation rate of 4% can be expected for individual consumers. If the "real" dividend growth level to stockholders is to be maintained, then the nominal rate must be increased from 6% to 10%. While this adjustment can be easily computed for each of the three examples presented in this section, there is reason to believe that such an adjustment would be inappropriate since presumably inflationary expectations have already been discounted by the market.